DATE DUE

MAR 0 6

GAYLORD			PRINTED IN U.S.A.

journalists
AT RISK

Why are journalists drawn to

the chaos of combat?...

[T]he allure is simple:

war is the biggest story of all.

—*Harold Evans,*
editor and author

journalists AT RISK

REPORTING AMERICA'S WARS

GEORGE SULLIVAN

TWENTY-FIRST CENTURY BOOKS · MINNEAPOLIS

Twenty-First Century Books
A division of Lerner Publishing Group
241 First Avenue North
Minneapolis, Minnesota 55401 U.S.A.

Website address: www.lernerbooks.com

Library of Congress Cataloging-in-Publication Data

Sullivan, George, 1927–
    Journalists at risk : reporting America's wars / George Sullivan.
        p.   cm. — (People's history)
    Summary: Discusses the role of reporters during war time, including the risks they take and the censorship they face, and how their jobs have changed with each conflict since the Civil War.
    Includes bibliographical references and index.
    ISBN-13: 978–0–7613–2745–5 (lib. bdg. : alk. paper)
    ISBN-10: 0–7613–2745–2 (lib. bdg. : alk. paper)
    1. War—Press coverage—United States. [1. War correspondents.
    2. Journalism.] I. Title. II. Series.
PN4784.W37 S85 2006
070.4'4935502—dc22   2003015855

Manufactured in the United States of America
1 2 3 4 5 6 – JR – 11 10 09 08 07 06

CONTENTS

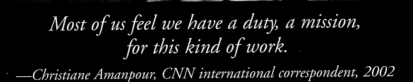

*Most of us feel we have a duty, a mission,
for this kind of work.*
—Christiane Amanpour, CNN international correspondent, 2002

FROM THE FRONT LINES

Wars are always big news. In times of armed conflict, people hunger for reports from the battlefronts. They want the news quickly. They want to see events as they take place. They want to read about them in their newspapers and magazines.

Ratings climb for television newscasts during wars. Newspaper circulations go up too. Men and women in distant places gather and report the news in times of war. These journalists bring their viewers, listeners, and readers stories of horror and heroism.

Their reports have to do not only with armed combat between nations. They send home stories of ethnic and religious strife. They also cover acts of terrorism.

In a democracy, it's important that the people be kept informed about events by full, fair, and accurate reporting. The knowledge gained enables citizens to understand the issues of the day. It helps them to choose the nation's leaders intelligently when they vote.

But many Americans question the news reports they see on TV or read in the newspapers and magazines. That's because some correspondents interpret the information that they gather. They often seek to influence their audiences. They "spin" the news. Correspondents once made more of an effort to do balanced reporting. "The old rules [of journalism] say you have no opinion, you simply report the news and let others decide," says Larry Sabato, author of *Feeding Frenzy: Attack Journalism and American Politics*.

In wartime it can be difficult for journalists to be open-minded or to write without bias. During the war in Iraq in 2003, for example, many liberal critics believed that the Bush administration made a shaky case for the war and that many correspondents failed to question the president's motives. Eric Alterman, a liberal media critic, said, "Support for the war is in part a reflection that the media has allowed the Bush administration to get away with misleading the American people." Conservative critics, on the other hand, accused some media outlets of being too critical of the president.

It has been the same in every war since the war in Vietnam (1957–1975). Some reporters are criticized for being too willing to trust the military. Other reporters are accused of being too critical of the war itself and of the military. It's a never-ending tug of war.

The Physical Dangers

Being a war correspondent sometimes involves great personal risk. In the United States, members of the media get the same legal protection as any civilian. But in some countries, the law is no safeguard.

Scores of journalists are killed every year. Hundreds are illegally imprisoned. Hundreds of others are physically attacked or subjected to threats against their safety.

It wasn't always like this. In days past, correspondents were rarely deliberately fired upon. The greatest risk came from being in the wrong place at the wrong time. Ernie Pyle, a popular correspondent during World War II (1939–1945), is one example. Pyle covered the fighting in North Africa, Sicily, Italy, and France. In the summer of 1944, he returned to the United States for a rest before moving on to the war's hot spots in the Pacific. The military did all it could to protect him. But Pyle died on the Pacific island of Ie Shima in 1945, the victim of enemy machine-gun fire.

During the war in Vietnam in the late 1960s, the situation began to change. Stray bullets were not the only problem.

This memorial on the island of Ie Shima in the western Pacific is where correspondent Ernie Pyle died during World War II, the victim of a sniper's bullet.

Correspondents were deliberately targeted by the enemy. By the end of the war, forty-five U.S. correspondents had been killed and eighteen were missing.

In recent years, reporting from war zones has become more dangerous than ever. Since 1992, dozens of journalists have been hunted down and murdered. These killings were often an effort to prevent the correspondents from doing further reporting or to punish them for what they had already reported.

Statistics gathered by the Committee to Protect Journalists, an independent organization that works to safeguard press freedom around the world, confirm this. In the decade beginning in 1992, a total of 389 journalists worldwide were killed while on the job. Of these, 289, or 77 percent, were murdered because of what they were reporting.

A stately locust tree serves as the war correspondents' memorial in Arlington National Cemetery in Washington, D.C. It honors "journalists who died while covering wars of conflict for the American people."

During the U.S. war on terrorism—which began after the attacks on the World Trade Center in New York and on the Pentagon near Washington, D.C., on September 11, 2001—journalists became the targets of Islamic extremists, many of whom believed that a close connection existed between U.S. journalists and the U.S. military. A reward of fifty thousand dollars was reported to have been offered for the murder of any U.S. or European journalist.

It shocked Americans when Pakistani militants kidnapped and executed Daniel Pearl, a correspondent for the *Wall Street Journal*, early in 2002. Pearl's murder was no isolated incident. During the month of December 2001 alone, seven journalists were killed while covering the war in Afghanistan.

Censoring the News

The physical danger in reporting from a war zone is likely to be a correspondent's greatest worry. But it's not the only one. Censorship is also a big issue.

The First Amendment to the U.S. Constitution says that "Congress shall make no law . . . abridging the freedom . . . of the press. . . ." This amendment makes it possible for U.S. journalists to carry out their assignments without interference from the government.

During wartime, however, the First Amendment can get over-looked. The freedom that the press usually enjoys often clashes with the military's demand for secrecy. For example, during the brief war in the Persian Gulf in 1991, journalists were made to operate under a strict system of controls set down by the military. Few correspondents got to the scene of the fighting. In the view of some, the public was not properly informed during the war.

In addition, during a war, information that might possibly give aid to the enemy gets withheld. For example, after the terrorist attacks on September 11, 2001, Ari Fleischer, President George W. Bush's press secretary, asked the media to follow certain guidelines. Don't share information on the president's schedule with the public, Fleischer said. He also asked correspondents not to report on how the United States gets its intelligence information.

It's no secret that the members of the military do not like to have war correspondents looking over their shoulders, reporting everything they see and hear. They don't want journalists reporting information that could be important to the enemy. Servicepeople could get killed as a result. The military is also fearful of having its mistakes revealed by journalists.

In an interview in 2002, Philip Knightley, the author of *The First Casualty,* an important history of war correspondents, explained how the military would like to treat the media. (The title of Knightley's book is from Senator Hiram Johnson, who, in 1917, remarked, "The first casualty when war comes is truth.") Knightley cited a meeting of censors, those who examine what journalists have written, during World War II.

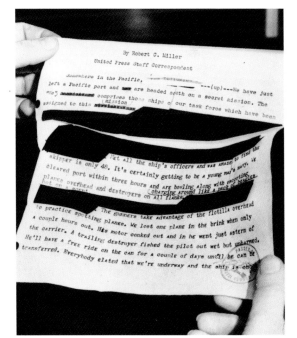

During World War II, correspondents had to cope with strict rules of censorship. This is a censored page from the notebook of United Press reporter Robert Miller, who covered that war.

"What should we tell the people about the war?" asked one of the censors.

"Well," said another, "let's tell them nothing until the war's over and then tell them who won."

Said Knightley: "That's the ideal as far as the military is concerned. . . ."

The problem of news censorship has become much more serious in recent times. New technology has revolutionized war reporting. A videophone with a satellite link enables a correspondent to send back live news accounts from any place, at any time. People have dubbed this new type of reporting backpack journalism. The hundreds, even thousands, of reporters covering a war can easily bury military censors in a great mass of information.

Greater controls can be the result. Reporters and broadcasters can be denied access to battle zones. Correspondents may then have no other choice but to get their information from press officers in conferences called briefings.

If war reporting is subject to such restrictions and at the same time is so perilous, why do so many men and women continue to do it? There are several reasons. To some, war reporting is exciting; it's an adventure. To others, war reporting is a noble cause.

"War correspondents are a different breed," says CNN's Christiane Amanpour. "Most of us believe that we have a duty, a mission, for this kind of work." When asked by her young son why she goes into war-torn countries to report on what's happening there, she tells him, "If I don't, the bad guys will win."

Still other journalists like war reporting because it can provide a quick path to professional success. Such television journalists as Christiane Amanpour and Peter Arnett saw their careers quickly boosted through their war coverage.

William "Billy" Russell of the *Times* (London) is often cited as the first war correspondent. About 150 years ago, Russell covered the Crimean War (1854–1856), revealing how the fighting men were in desperate need of medicine and clothing. Russell referred to himself as the first of a "luckless tribe." Decades later, the tribe is still in the field.

*Great Battle!
Near Manassas
Junction!...
Bravery of the
Federal Troops.
The Rebels
Completely
Routed*

—error-filled Civil
War telegram, First
Battle of Bull Run in
Virginia, 1861

NEWS BY WIRE

Just as warfare has changed over the years—from soldiers on horseback armed with swords and rifles to the use of such weapons as drone planes and smart bombs—so have the ways of covering it. In the Revolutionary War (1775–1783) and the War of 1812 (1812–1815), news traveled very slowly. Battlefront reports were handwritten. They were hand delivered too, often by messengers on horseback. Any dispatch sent over a long distance could travel no faster than the fastest horse.

Great change came with the telegraph, the use of which dates from the late 1830s. A system of sending messages by means of wires and electric current, the telegraph quickly became the chief method of transmitting news stories.

No longer did newspaper readers have to be satisfied with news that was a week old. With the telegraph, an event that happened one day could appear as a news story the next. Newspaper reporters called the telegraph "the lightning" because of how quickly it transmitted what they had written.

In 1848 the telegraph led to the founding of the first news service. Six newspapers in New York City formed an organization that gathered the news and then transmitted dispatches to newspapers in other parts of the country, collecting a fee for the service. They called their enterprise the Associated Press (AP), and it has become the world's largest news service.

War with Mexico

The telegraph played a role, although a limited one, in the Mexican-American War (1846–1848). That war represented one of the first efforts by American journalists to deliver reports directly from foreign battlefields to newspapers back home.

The war had a number of causes, most dating from 1835 when Texans revolted against the government of Mexico and, a year later, established the Republic of Texas. The government of Mexico would not recognize Texas as an independent nation. When Texas became part of the United States in 1845, it deepened Mexico's anger. The nation broke off diplomatic relations with the United States. The disputed border between Mexico and the United States also helped to trigger the outbreak of war.

When President James K. Polk sent troops to invade northern Mexico and to capture Mexico City and Veracruz, reporters went with them. They followed the campaigns closely, sending their dispatches by steamboat to New Orleans. From there, the stories were sent to newspapers in Atlanta, Washington, New York, and Boston.

In 1847 U.S. troops landed on the beaches during the Battle of Veracruz. George Kendall's boat was also moored in Veracruz, enabling him to get eyewitness accounts of the action during the Mexican-American War.

George Kendall, founder of the *New Orleans Picayune,* made a special effort to speed war news to his readers. Kendall purchased a small, fast steamer and outfitted the vessel with typesetting machines and printing presses. Messengers on horseback took reporters' accounts of battles to the port of Veracruz where Kendall's steamship waited. On board, Kendall's men printed the news so that it was ready to send out to the reading public the moment his vessel docked in New Orleans.

The Treaty of Guadalupe Hidalgo ended the war on February 2, 1848. (The treaty also enabled the United States to acquire lands that became the states of California, Nevada, and Utah, and parts of Arizona, New Mexico, Colorado, and Wyoming.)

In getting news of the treaty back to the United States, George Kendall again beat all of his rivals. Thanks to the efforts of Kendall and other U.S. reporters and editors, historian Robert Henry has been able to cite the Mexican War as "the first war in history to be adequately and comprehensively reported in the daily press."

The Civil War

When the Civil War (1861–1865) erupted, it created an enormous demand for news. Newspapers of the day went to great lengths in an effort to satisfy that demand. Northern newspapers employed some five hundred correspondents during the war. The *New York Herald* alone had sixty-three reporters in the field.

The nation's telegraph system had grown rapidly following the Mexican-American War. In 1853, only five years after the war had ended, 23,000 miles (37,014 kilometers) of telegraph wire had been strung throughout the United States. By 1860, a total of 50,000 miles (80,465 kilometers) of telegraph lines were in use. The system linked most major cities.

While the telegraph made it possible for news stories to get to the public faster, what was written was of poor quality. In *The First Casualty,* Knightley describes Civil War reporters as "ignorant, dishonest, and unethical." He calls their news stories "frequently inaccurate, often invented. . . ." Henry Villard, a correspondent for the *New York Herald,* agreed. He remarked: "Men turned up as correspondents more fit to drive cattle than write for newspapers."

Dedicated to Civil War correspondents and artists, this impressive memorial stands in Gathland State Park near Burkittsville, Maryland. (It also honors journalists who died covering wars in the early 2000s.)

Correspondents put little emphasis on being accurate. The first Battle of Bull Run, in July 1861, is one example. When Union forces began attacking the outmanned Confederates, reporters from the papers in the North saw a great Union victory in the making. They hurried back to Washington, only about 30 miles (48 kilometers) away, to send news of the Union army's success to their readers. But the Southern troops, bolstered by reinforcements, held the line and then charged the Northerners. The Northerners fell back in a rout. Because reporters had acted too hastily, a stunning defeat for the North was reported as a glorious victory in New York newspapers.

Bull Run was only one example of sloppy work. Battlefield casualties were often underreported by correspondents. At times, the entire Southern army was said to be marching on Washington. Atlanta was reported to have been captured a week before the event actually happened. A reporter for the *New York Tribune* wrote a dramatic account of the Battle of Pea Ridge, Arkansas. Although highly praised, the article turned out to be wholly fictional.

The South did no better. Instead of professional reporters, Southern newspapers often relied on army officers who volunteered to send reports by letter or telegram when they had the time to do so. These war dispatches were routinely glaring in their support of the Southern cause.

A good number of photographers also covered the Civil War. But the photographs they took were largely unseen by the public. That's because popular publications of the 1860s did not have the technology to reproduce photographs for their readers. Not until the 1880s did newspapers gain the technical know-how that enabled them to accurately reproduce a photographic image.

In the years following the Civil War, new technologies triggered a period of great industrial growth in America. Newspaper publishing was deeply affected. In 1886 the *New York Tribune* became the first newspaper to use a Linotype machine. An operator sitting at a keyboard could produce solid lines of type from which the newspaper was printed. Previously, type had to be set by hand, one letter at a time.

The dead Confederates are gathered here for burial following the 1863 Battle of Gettysburg. Such photographs were not uncommon during the Civil War. More recently, photographs of battlefield dead have been considered disrespectful and have often been censored by the U.S. government.

By the turn of the century, the gathering and reporting of the news had been made easier and more efficient by the wide use of the telephone, which had been developed during the 1870s. The portable typewriter, which first appeared in 1909, was another step forward.

At the time, William Randolph Hearst reigned as the nation's most powerful publisher. After he inherited San Francisco's *Examiner* from his father, Hearst founded or bought one newspaper after another. By the beginning of the 1900s, Hearst owned a chain of nine newspapers. He also published two magazines. To make his publications popular with the readers, Hearst relied on his belief that "the public is even more fond of entertainment than it is of information."

In New York City, Hearst's *Journal* was locked in a fierce struggle for circulation with the *World,* published by Joseph Pulitzer. In their intense rivalry, the two papers fed their readers sensationalism—stories of crime, natural disasters, and scandal.

War with Spain

During this period of journalistic combat and growth, the Spanish-American War (1898) erupted. The war was an outgrowth of a rebellion in Cuba, then a colony of Spain. The Cubans rose up against Spanish rule.

Reporters for Hearst and Pulitzer were deeply involved in the situation. Richard Harding Davis, an action-loving correspondent for the *New York Journal*, had been covering the story for almost two years. Davis believed that the United States should step in and help the Cuban rebels. His stories mirrored that point of view. Davis was fully supported by Hearst.

Hearst realized that big headlines and lively stories dealing with events in Cuba could win many thousands of new readers for the *Journal*. Truth and accuracy weren't important to Hearst. When the U.S. battleship *Maine* suffered an explosion that led to its sinking in Havana Harbor early in 1898, the Spanish said it was an accident. Not Hearst and the *Journal*. The newspaper, without a shred of evidence, blamed Spain. The *Journal* declared that the sinking of the *Maine* was due to "an enemy's secret infernal machine."

In the weeks that followed, Hearst's *Journal* ran one sensational story after another, whipping up public enthusiasm for the war. Correspondents with famous names were sent to Cuba to write the stories. What they wrote was heralded by headlines in four-inch type. "Remember the *Maine*!" became a national catch phrase. Before the end of April, Congress, greatly influenced by public opinion, passed a formal declaration of war.

Most of the war's fighting was done in Cuba and the Philippines. When the conflict ended, Cuba got its independence. The United States claimed Puerto Rico, Guam, and the Philippines.

The destruction of the Maine—*and the* New York Journal's *misreporting that it was the work of Spain—helped start the Spanish-American War of 1898.*

William Randolph Hearst got what he wanted too. He saw sales of the *Journal* double and redouble and eventually reach one million copies a day.

Worldwide War

Unlike the Spanish-American War, World War I (1914–1918) was a truly global conflict. It involved more countries and caused more destruction than any war in history up to that time.

The Allied nations at the outset of World War I included Great Britain, France, and Russia (until 1917). Italy joined the Allies in 1915. As enemy nations, the Allies faced Germany, Austria-Hungary, Turkey, and, in 1915, Bulgaria. These nations were known as the Central Powers.

In the early months of the war, the Germans advanced through Belgium into France, almost as far as Paris. Then the German attack stalled along what came to be known as the western front. The two opposing armies representing the Allies and the Central Powers dug a network of trenches from which they launched attacks and defended their positions. Trench warfare dragged on for four more years.

From the earliest days of the war, correspondents from U.S. newspapers traveled to Europe hoping to cover events. They joined reporters from other neutral countries, such as Denmark, Sweden, Switzerland, and the Netherlands. News dispatches from Europe could be quickly transmitted to the United States by means of the Atlantic telegraph cable. (The transatlantic cable had been in operation since 1866.)

Many of the U.S. correspondents in Europe were working for news services, which had expanded in importance. In 1907 Edward Scripps, owner of a newspaper chain, founded a news agency that later became the United Press International. United Press competed with the Associated Press. William Randolph Hearst established the International News Service two years later. Before the end of the century, the Associated Press would be providing news to more than fifteen hundred daily newspapers and many thousands of broadcast outlets.

The news agencies were known as wire services because they sent news reports to their member papers over telegraph wires. Later, when telegraph wires were replaced by more modern means of transmitting information, AP, UP, and INS became known as news services.

William Shepherd of the United Press was one of the first U.S. correspondents to produce a scoop, that is, to reveal an important piece of news before any of his rivals. On a spring morning in April 1915, Shepherd was nearby when the Germans unleashed their first poison-gas attack.

At the time, the war's opposing forces were locked in a propaganda battle to win the backing of the United States. Shepherd's story describing the use of poison gas by the Germans and the suffering of

During World War I, Germany was the first to use poisonous gas as a weapon of war. William Shepherd's horrible 1915 accounts of victims coughing and choking hurt Germany's standing in the United States.

the victims filled his American readers with horror. It hurt Germany's efforts to gain the support of the United States.

In the fall of 1915, Shepherd was the author of another remarkable scoop. The Germans used huge airships, called zeppelins, to bomb London. Shepherd was present during the first zeppelin attack on London. He described how the people of London "fought fires, rescued wounded, shrugged off an entirely new type of warfare and patching together their houses and shops carried on as usual." Americans could not help but be impressed by the heroics of the Londoners.

The American people had no wish to get involved in the war, however. They considered the conflict to be a European matter. A turning point came on May 17, 1915, when a German U-boat torpedoed and sank the British liner *Lusitania*. The sinking brought death to 1,198 people, including 128 Americans. Although classified as a passenger ship, the *Lusitania* was carrying munitions, it was later revealed. The sinking of the *Lusitania* came to be looked upon as an anti-American

On May 7, 1915, a German U-boat torpedoed the British ocean liner Lusitania. Although more than one hundred Americans lost their lives, the United States stayed out of World War I for two more years.

act. That tragedy, plus other shipping losses, helped to lead the United States into the conflict on the side of the Allies.

U.S. troops began arriving in Europe in 1917. Immediately, the demand sharpened for battlefront news. People back home wanted to know what was happening to their husbands, sons, and brothers.

Nevertheless, U.S. journalists had to cope with a rigid set of controls. Correspondents had to appear in person before the secretary of war or his representative and swear to "convey the truth to the people of the United States." Newspapers had to pay one thousand dollars to the army to cover the cost of each correspondent's equipment and other expenses. Newspapers also had to post a ten-thousand-dollar bond for each correspondent. If the reporter failed to follow the rules, the money was to be forfeited.

Reporters on the scene in Europe found that their stories were seldom allowed to pass as they were written. Military censors argued that the facts they contained could aid the enemy.

Floyd Gibbons, who reported for the *Chicago Tribune* and was well known as a war correspondent, rebelled at the censorship restrictions. He was always looking for the real action. In June 1918, Gibbons joined U.S. units in their attack on German forces in Belleau Wood, a forested area on the Marne River, east of Paris. During an exchange of gunfire, Gibbons took shelter in a trench. The firing stopped, and Gibbons poked his head up to see what was happening. A bullet ripped into his shoulder. Another pierced his left eye.

Gibbons recovered in a Paris hospital. Afterward, the white eye patch he wore became his trademark and helped to earn him celebrity status. During the fall of 1918, the superior Allied forces won one important victory after another. The war ended on November 11, 1918, when Germany agreed to armistice terms and the fighting stopped.

The telegraph continued as a vital means of sending messages over long distances until the mid-1900s. For almost a full century of the nation's history, "the lightning" was the chief means of sending news and other information from one distant point to another. But the telegraph was eventually overshadowed by radio and other methods of transmitting speech and other sounds over long distances without the use of wires.

Floyd Gibbons lost an eye as he was covering World War I for the Chicago Tribune.

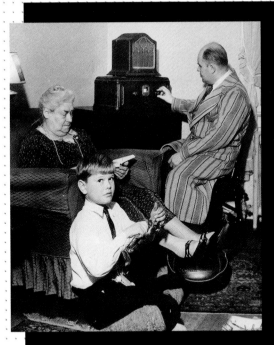

We interrupt this program to bring you a special news bulletin. The Japanese have attacked Pearl Harbor.
—John Daly, CBS announcer, December 1941

"REMEMBER PEARL HARBOR!"

During the 1920s and 1930s, the world of news reporting went through a period of revolutionary change, and radio was the reason. Radio went from being mostly an experimental service to becoming the largest mass medium in the United States. Radio ushered in the age of broadcast journalism.

Before radio, the telegraph and the telephone were the chief means of long-distance communication. But both of these could be used only between places that were connected by wires. Radio was different. Radio did not require wires. Radio signals passed through the air.

With radio, people could communicate between any two points on the land, on the sea, or in the air. Radio thus meant that people could hear news reports from anywhere in the world as they actually happened or within seconds afterward.

Radio experienced spectacular growth during the 1920s. Pittsburgh's KDKA transmitted the presidential election results on November 2, 1920. (Warren G. Harding won.) The broadcast marked the beginning of radio journalism in the United States.

Radio stations soon popped up everywhere. By 1923 more than five hundred stations were in operation. By 1929 more than twelve million families had radios.

Just as in the newspaper field, groups of radio stations banded together to form chains, or, as they came to be called, networks. A network was made up of dozens or even hundreds of stations linked by wire and, later, by microwave relays. This meant the same program could be broadcast simultaneously to all of the network's listeners. The National Broadcasting Company (NBC) formed the first radio network in 1926. The Columbia Broadcasting System (CBS) began operation a year later.

By the late 1930s, radio was approaching its popularity peak. About 85 percent of all American households had radios. Millions listened regularly to Jack Benny, Fred Allen, and Bob Hope, who were, perhaps, the most well-known Americans of the time.

Reporting World War II

At this time, World War II was brewing in Europe. And radio news correspondents were there. The war that they reported upon was the most far-reaching and destructive in history. Military operations in World War I were limited mostly to Europe. But in World War II, more than fifty countries took part. Bitter fighting took place not only in Europe but also in Asia, North Africa, the North Atlantic, and the island areas of the central and southwest Pacific.

Germany, Japan, and Italy were among the chief participants. They were known as the Axis powers. The United States, Great Britain, the the Union of Soviet Socialist Republics (USSR), China, and France opposed the Axis powers and their aggression.

On September 1, 1939, Germany attacked Poland. Featuring a new kind of war called blitzkrieg, or "lightning war," the German army's fast tanks and armored vehicles raced across Poland. At the same time, German planes called Stukas rained bombs on Polish troops. Heavier planes bombed Polish cities. Polish resistance quickly melted. In April 1940, Germany struck again. This time Norway and Denmark were the targets. German soldiers met little resistance. When France surrendered later in June, Germany was in control of all of northern Europe.

The Germans boasted that they would be in London before the end of the summer. To prepare for the invasion of Great Britain, German

When German bombers began to attack London in 1940, millions of children were moved out of the city to the safety of the countryside.

Edward R. Murrow, radio correspondent for CBS, in 1939

bombers began to pound British ports and airfields. London was often a target. The British fought back gallantly. Royal Air Force pilots at the controls of fast Spitfire and Hurricane fighters shot down hundreds of enemy bombers. Their losses were so severe that the Germans gave up the idea of invading Great Britain. But the bombing continued.

During these early stages of World War II, the United States was not yet involved. But U.S. correspondents were in Europe reporting what they heard and saw. Several hundred reporters worked in Europe for the news services, for Associated Press, United Press, and International News Service. In addition, major U.S. newspapers had correspondents throughout Europe.

Of the many radio broadcasters who reported from Europe in the early years of the war, none was better known or more listened to than Edward R. Murrow. It was during the Blitz, the relentless German bombing of London in 1940, that Murrow and his rich, expressive voice first came to the attention of U.S. radio audiences. He had convinced CBS of the importance of having radio reporters offer eyewitness accounts as they unfolded. His broadcasts during the Battle of Britain included the sounds of air-raid sirens and bombs exploding. On at least one occasion, Murrow broadcast from the roof of a London building during a raid to give a firsthand account of what the British were being made to endure.

U.S. foreign policy had traditionally stressed noninvolvement in European affairs. Despite the fact that German bombers were devastating London, millions of Americans still wished to continue a policy of isolation. Murrow's broadcasts helped Americans to understand that the free world was in desperate need of help from the United States and that entering the war might be necessary.

At about the same time that German and British aircraft were brawling in the skies over Britain, the war was spreading. Italian troops, supported by Hitler's Afrika Korps, attacked British forces in North Africa. German troops in Europe overran Yugoslavia, then moved on to Greece, and soon controlled all of the Balkan nations.

In June 1941, Hitler ordered an attack on the Soviet Union, sending three million troops across the long Soviet border. German troops got within sight of Moscow, the Soviet capital. Then the Soviets began pushing back the Germans.

U.S. Involvement

Americans, meanwhile, remained divided on whether the United States should join the fight. While most Americans supported the Allies, there was strong opposition to sending U.S. troops overseas. This largely changed after December 7, 1941.

For most Americans, the day began as a normal, quiet Sunday. After attending church and enjoying a big midday meal, many families settled down for an afternoon of leisure. There was the Sunday paper to read. Later, they might take the car out for a drive or listen to the radio. (Television was not yet in most homes.) No one dreamed that this would be the last Sunday for almost four years that the country would be at peace.

At the White House, President Franklin D. Roosevelt looked forward to a quiet lunch in his study with his friend and adviser Harry Hopkins. Mrs. Roosevelt busied herself with a luncheon for some relatives and friends.

In New York City, the New York Philharmonic, the oldest symphony orchestra in the United States, assembled for its regular Sunday afternoon concert. Not long after 2:00 P.M., conductor Artur Rodzinsky raised his baton, and the performance began with the playing of the Symphony No. 1 in F Minor by Russian composer Dmitry Shostakovich. The CBS radio network offered the concert to listeners across the nation.

As the playing of Shostakovich's composition was nearing the end, an anxious voice broke in. "We interrupt this program to bring you a special bulletin," an announcer said. "The Japanese have attacked Pearl Harbor, Hawaii, by air, President Roosevelt has just announced. The attack was also made on all naval and military activities on the principal island of Oahu."

A similar bulletin was broadcast by the Mutual Broadcasting System, the network that was carrying the New York Giants-Brooklyn Dodgers football game. Most Americans heard these news flashes on their living room radios. Or they heard them on their car radios or at filling stations when they stopped for gas. Americans continued to rely on radio for the up-to-the-minute news in the war years that followed.

Newspapers were still vitally important, of course. People would get most of their detailed information about the war from reading newspapers. But radio, by being first with the news, would play a leading role.

The shock of the attack on Pearl Harbor ended the opposition. The event united Americans as nothing before. The next day, Congress approved a declaration of war against Japan. Thousands of Americans rushed to enlist in the armed services. And everywhere, "Remember Pearl Harbor!" was the rallying cry.

World War II Up Close

As soon as the United States officially entered World War II, a flood of U.S. journalists crossed the Atlantic to report on the conflict. Many of them wore the uniforms of U.S. officers. The letter *C*, for correspondent, was sewn on the uniform's right sleeve. Since the journalists looked like officers, they were sometimes treated by the military as just another branch of the armed services.

Correspondents found censorship overseas to be stricter than it had been in the United States. They were not allowed into war zones unless they were accredited. That meant that each reporter had to meet official requirements set down by the U.S. military. Most important, each correspondent had to sign an agreement to submit the text of his or her news stories to a military censor. The censor could cut out pieces of information or kill every word.

Ernie Pyle, the foremost columnist of the war, reported on the Allied campaign in North Africa and remained with the Allied forces during their invasion of Sicily and Italy. Pyle did his reporting from the front lines. He saw World War II through the eyes of the war's regular Joes—the GIs. He lived with them, bunked in the same quarters, and ate the same food. He tramped on dirt roads with them. He traveled to almost every battle area in North Africa and Europe before switching to the Pacific Theater of Operations.

Pyle's column, which appeared in about four hundred daily newspapers, was something like a soldier's letter to the folks back home. He talked about hard beds, lousy food, and the lack of sleep. He also told of the terror of warfare and the numbness that soldiers felt with death and destruction all around them.

"I love the infantry because they are the underdogs," Pyle said in an interview that appeared in the *New York World Telegram* in 1943. "They are the mud-rain-frost-and-wind boys. They have no comforts and they even learn to live without necessities, and in the end they are the guys that wars can't be won without."

The sergeants and privates that Pyle wrote about were not nameless.

Ernie Pyle (**third from left**) *on the trail with a group of U.S. Marines on Okinawa in 1945*

Pyle reported soldiers' names, their cities and towns, and sometimes even their street addresses. No doubt this increased his popularity among enlisted men.

Pyle seldom had any difficulty with censors. The military loved him. They realized that he was good for morale. Said General Omar Bradley: "Our soldiers always seemed to fight a little better when Ernie was around."

Women in the War Zone

Edward R. Murrow wasn't the only U.S. correspondent reporting from London during the summer of 1940 when the city was a nightly target for German bombers. Helen Kirkpatrick, a reporter for the *Chicago Daily News,* was also on the scene. In ambulances and

Women war correspondents in London in 1943 (from left): *Mary Welch,* Time *and* Life; *Dixie Tighe,* International News Service; *Kathleen Harriman,* Newsweek; *Helen Kirkpatrick,* Chicago Daily News; *Lee Miller,* Vogue; *and Tania Long, the* New York Times

fire engines and sometimes on her bicycle, Kirkpatrick would ride through the ravaged streets of the city. Her articles in the *Daily News* reported her thoughts and feelings to her readers. What Kirkpatrick produced was described by historian Frederick Voss as "some of the best coverage in the American press of that phase of World War II."

Margaret Bourke-White, one of a handful of original photographers hired by the picture magazine *Life,* was another of the first female journalists to cover World War II. She was in Moscow in the summer of 1941 when the first German bombs rained upon Moscow. Her pictures were an exciting scoop for *Life* and Bourke-White.

For the next four years, Bourke-White covered the war in Europe. She documented the campaigns in North Africa and Italy in 1942 and 1943. She followed the Allied push into Germany in the spring of 1945. As the first woman to be issued official credentials by the U.S. Army Air Force, she flew on bombing raids, taking pictures of the destruction.

While it is not unusual today for a woman to report the news from a battle zone, in the 1940s, it was. Men alone did the fighting in the 1940s. To most people of the time, it made sense that men should do the war reporting too. Women, men said, were too fragile and too emotional to be war correspondents. There were too many hardships. The work was believed to be too dangerous for them. It was wrong for women to attempt to endure bombings and strafings, sniper fire, and primitive living conditions. Tad Bartimus, who wrote a nationally syndicated column for women, cited another problem. It was what she called The Big Excuse or The Bathroom Thing. Women, it was said, couldn't travel to battle zones because there was no place for them to properly relieve themselves.

The Big Excuse is not an issue today. "Women covering wars don't worry about such things," said Bartimus recently. "Female journalists, like their male counterparts, worry about getting the facts right, getting the story out, beating the competition and surviving to tell another tale. We are resourceful or we wouldn't be in this business."

The Right to Know

The surprise attack on Pearl Harbor lasted nearly two hours. When the Japanese planes roared off to return to their aircraft carriers, the U.S. fleet lay in ruins, and 2,403 U.S. soldiers, sailors, marines, and civilians were dead. Five U.S. battleships had been sunk, and three had been damaged. Three cruisers and three destroyers were put out of action. About two hundred planes were destroyed.

But no American newspaper or radio network reported the U.S. losses. The U.S. government kept that news secret from the public. Almost from the moment that the first bomb exploded, the war's news coverage was censored.

Secretary of the Navy Frank Knox and Secretary of War Harry Stimson aided in the cover-up of the U.S. Navy's losses at Pearl Harbor. In this cartoon from 1941, an irritated Uncle Sam urges the pair ". . . to tell the people the facts."

The official statement issued after the attack reported that only one battleship and a destroyer had been sunk and other ships damaged. The report also said that the Japanese had suffered many casualties. (The Japanese lost only 24 of the 360 aircraft in the raid.)

Several days after the attack, Frank Knox, secretary of the navy, flew to Hawaii to conduct an inspection tour of Pearl Harbor. Afterward, he held a news conference. He told reporters that only one U.S. battleship, the *Arizona,* had been lost. He also said that the battleship *Oklahoma* had been overturned but that the vessel could be righted and returned to service. He did not say that the battleships *California, Nevada,* and *West Virginia* were resting on the bottom of the Pearl Harbor anchorage. The full truth about what happened at Pearl Harbor was not revealed until after the war ended.

Why the cover-up? Knox and other government officials feared that the American public would not be able to accept the truth. To reveal how serious a blow the nation had suffered, they believed, would be doing great harm to the morale of the American public and the armed forces.

There was another factor. The U.S. Army and Navy had been caught off guard at Pearl Harbor. By misleading the press, the military hoped to be able to conceal its blunders.

Later it was argued that the refusal to admit U.S. losses was necessary to keep the Japanese from knowing the disastrous results of the attack. But the Japanese knew exactly what they had accomplished. In the days following the attack, Japanese newspapers in Tokyo gave an accurate report of the number of U.S. ships put out of action and other U.S. losses.

Censoring within the United States

During World War II, military censorship of the media took different forms. Within the United States itself, the government set up an Office of Censorship in Washington. Byron Price, a former correspondent and executive for the Associated Press, headed the operation.

Price established a system of censorship that was largely voluntary. He issued a set of guidelines for curbing certain news stories. He encouraged the country's newspapers, radio stations, and magazines to follow them.

The guidelines were based on a question that Price wanted reporters and editors to ask in reviewing any story that seemed subject to being censored. The question was: "Is this information I would like to have if I were the enemy?" If the answer happened to be no, then the story could be printed or broadcast. If the answer was yes, the story was to be killed. If maybe was the answer, then Price advised the newspaper or radio station to consult the Office of Censorship for advice.

The guidelines issued by the Office of Censorship suggested certain topics that the media should steer clear of. These included stories of troop movements or weapons production. The media were also asked to avoid mentioning the precise location of army camps and navy bases.

The weather was another concern. Information about storms—or the absence of them—could be valuable to an enemy planning an attack on the United States or Allied shipping off the U.S. coasts. Thus, newspapers and radio stations were asked to drop their weather reports.

Censorship also had to do with photographs. For the first two years of the war, no photographs of U.S. soldiers or sailors who had died as a result of enemy action could be released to the public. In 1943 the government decided that the public should no longer be shielded from the war's realities, and the restriction was relaxed. Images of bodies were released to the newspapers. But photographs showing the faces of the dead were still considered too realistic. The ban on such photos was never lifted.

Censoring African American Newspapers

When it came to censorship, what was then called the "Negro press" presented a special problem to the military. The Negro press referred to those two hundred or so newspapers that were published especially for African American readers. The major ones included the *Baltimore Afro-American,* the *Norfolk Journal and Guide,* the *Houston Informer,* the *Chicago Daily Defender,* the *Pittsburgh Courier,* and the *New York Amsterdam News.*

In 1941, when the United States entered World War II, the armed forces were segregated. African American soldiers and sailors were kept separate from white units. Black units were assigned white commanding officers. Even the military's blood supply for the wounded was kept separate by race.

Tens of thousands of African Americans served willingly in the U.S. Army, Navy, and Marine Corps. Yet many African American soldiers and sailors had mixed feelings about what they were doing. They wondered how they could serve in the armed forces, perhaps even sacrifice their lives, while segregation remained.

Mainstream newspapers largely ignored the issue. But African American publishers and journalists criticized the government's policy of military segregation. The Associated Press, a news service that supplied black newspapers with news and opinion columns, also championed the cause of full citizenship for African Americans.

What was called the Double V campaign helped to keep alive the topic of segregation. The campaign got its start when a young cafeteria worker named James Thompson wrote a letter to the *Pittsburgh Courier.* In the letter, Thompson declared that he was troubled by the idea that he might be called into the military to defend a nation in which he was treated like a second-class citizen.

Thompson suggested that African Americans take up a Double V campaign. One of the *V*s was to stand for victory in the war over enemies "from without," that is, the Axis powers. The other *V* was to

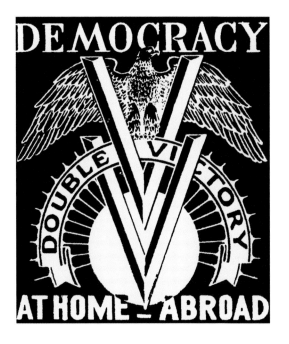

During World War II, this emblem became the symbol of the Double V campaign. One V *stood for victory over Germany, Japan, and the other Axis powers. The second* V *represented victory over prejudice.*

represent victory at home against the enemy of prejudice from within. The news columns of the *Pittsburgh Courier* and other African American newspapers enthusiastically supported the effort. Before long, there were Double V stickers, lapel pins, songs, and even hairstyles.

All of this made the military very nervous. Officials worried that the Double V campaign and the coverage of it by the Negro press could dampen their support of the war. The military reacted harshly. Military authorities seized and burned African American newspapers to keep them out of the hands of African American soldiers. African American newspapers were banned from military libraries.

Ollie Stewart, whose dispatches appeared regularly in the *Baltimore Afro-American* beginning in 1941, was the most notable African American journalist of World War II. He was the first African American to cover the war from North Africa and Europe. In 1943, when President Franklin D. Roosevelt met with British prime minister Winston Churchill to plan the invasions of southern and western Europe, Stewart was the only African American journalist to report on the event. He also covered the Tuskegee Airmen. This famed all-African American flying unit trained at the Tuskegee Institute in Tuskegee, Alabama, and became the 99th Pursuit (later Fighter) Squadron. The Tuskegee Airmen flew more than fifteen hundred combat missions over North Africa and Europe.

The African American press drove J. Edgar Hoover, director of the FBI, to fury. He believed that the Double V campaign would lead to rebellion against the government. Hoover wanted to have African American publishers tried for treason—that is, for helping the nation's enemies. Attorney General Francis Biddle, however, was able to curb Hoover's efforts.

Despite the actions of the U.S. government, African American newspapers enjoyed a period of great success during World War II. Throughout the war, these newspapers served, as Martin Luther King Jr. was later to say, as "one major voice of conscience of the nation."

Censorship in the Pacific

In the Pacific Theater of Operations, as in Europe, correspondents had to endure strict rules of censorship. One of these rules stated that each accredited journalist had to submit his or her copy to military censors for approval. The two groups were in constant conflict. Correspondents sought to report as much as possible. Censors wanted them to tell as little as possible.

The Battle of Midway, one of the decisive victories of the war for the United States, is one example. In June 1942, Japan's goal was to seize Midway Island, a tiny speck in the Pacific about 1,000 miles (1,609 kilometers) northwest of Hawaii.

The Japanese did not know it, but the United States had broken Japan's secret military code. As a result, U.S. naval forces in the Pacific knew Japan's plans in advance. The navy rushed every available airplane and warship to the Midway area.

The naval battle lasted four days, from June 3 to 6, 1942. Both sides suffered heavy losses. But for the Japanese, Midway was a very serious and far-reaching defeat. Not only did the Japanese fail to capture Midway Island, but their navy lost four aircraft carriers, two heavy cruisers, and three destroyers. (The U.S. Navy lost one carrier.) Japan also lost control of the central Pacific.

No U.S. correspondents were on hand to witness the battle. News stories of the victory were sketchy at best. And the navy was not interested in reporting in detail what had happened at Midway. Navy officials feared that the full story of the battle could be damaging. It might enable the Japanese to realize that their code had been cracked.

Stanley Johnston, a correspondent for the *Chicago Tribune,* was unaware of this. Johnston happened to be returning to the United States aboard a naval transport. Sailors on the vessel kept telling him of the big naval battle that was under way at Midway Island.

When he got back to Chicago, Johnston wrote a long article based upon what he had learned from the sailors. It turned out to be a remarkably accurate account of what had taken place, describing the

Stanley Johnston, correspondent for the Chicago Tribune

Japanese fleet in great detail. The article appeared on the front page of the *Tribune* on June 7.

When navy officials saw the story, they seethed with anger. Surely the Japanese now knew that their codes were useless. Johnston was called to Washington to be questioned. Some navy officials talked of having him brought to trial for spying.

Johnston couldn't understand why the navy was so upset. All he wanted to do, he said, was report a great U.S. naval victory. Although he never was punished in any way, he was bitter over his treatment by the navy.

Death Camp Impressions

During the early months of 1945, Allied troops pressed into the heart of Germany from all directions. Germany's official surrender came a week later. The date, May 8, 1945, was celebrated as V-E (for Victory in Europe) Day.

Martha Gellhorn, a pioneering female journalist, heard the news of Germany's surrender while she was at the notorious death camp near Dachau. She had arrived there with Allied troops a few days earlier. Dachau, Gellhorn said, seemed to be "the most suitable place in Europe" to learn of the Allied victory. "Surely this war was made

U.S. troops—as well as Martha Gellhorn and Marguerite Higgins—were among the first war correspondents to see the liberation of Jews from the death camp at Dachau in 1945.

to abolish Dachau," she said. "And all the other places like Dachau, and everything that Dachau stood for, and to abolish it forever."

Martha Gellhorn was not the only female correspondent to witness the liberation of Dachau. Twenty-five-year-old Marguerite Higgins of the *New York Herald-Tribune* was there too. Whereas Gellhorn was at the top of her profession, Higgins was beginning her ascent. Before long, she would reign as a journalism superstar.

Higgins wanted to go overseas as a war correspondent for the paper. She believed she was very well qualified. She had won high praise from her newspaper for her aggressive reporting and solid writing. But her request for assignment to Europe was denied. Women were not sent overseas. That was the newspaper's policy. Higgins wouldn't accept the ruling. She went to see Helen Reid, publisher of the *Herald-Tribune,* and pleaded her case.

Marguerite Higgins of the New York Herald-Tribune *won renown for her coverage of World War II. She later reported from battle zones in Korea and Vietnam.*

Not long after, Higgins was assigned to the newspaper's London bureau. That didn't satisfy her. She wanted to get closer to the battlefront. She managed to get transferred to Paris in March 1945 and began reporting from inside Germany. She wrote graphic stories of starving civilians and wounded soldiers. She was at Buchenwald, one of the largest of the Nazi death camps, soon after Allied soldiers had liberated the prisoners held there.

Later she went to Dachau. An American army officer tried to convince her not to enter the camp. "Don't you realize the place is raging with typhus?" he said. "Get out of here." "I've had my typhus shot," Higgins declared. "Lay off me! I'm doing my job!"

People were aware that the death camps existed. British newspapers had reported that more than one million Jews had been killed in the camps since the beginning of the war. But few people knew of the horror of the camps. Higgins sought to convey that reality to her readers.

In her account of the camp's liberation, Higgins told how the newly freed prisoners beat one of the guards to death. She also reported how the liberated prisoners reacted when they were placed in isolation to be screened for typhus. Higgins told how the prisoners

"...flung themselves against the electrically-charged fences, electrocuting themselves before our eyes."

When Higgins returned to New York City, she was named the best foreign correspondent of 1945 by the New York Newspaper Women's Club. Higgins came to be recognized as one of the best-known and most respected U.S. journalists. No reporter did more to advance the cause of equal access for women as war correspondents.

Off-Limits in Japan

General Douglas MacArthur, chief of Allied ground forces in the Pacific, imposed the toughest censorship regulations of any theater of war. Correspondents were not permitted to interview any member of the Allied forces. One who did so would be punished. Any soldier

General Douglas MacArthur (center), *chief of Allied ground forces in the Pacific during World War II, kept the press under tight control.*

who granted an interview would be court-martialed. All news stories had to be cleared by MacArthur's headquarters.

MacArthur was very much concerned with his reputation. He wanted to be portrayed as a military genius, the architect of the Allied victory to come. Articles in any way critical of MacArthur were often killed. Censors also frowned upon news stories that focused on Allied casualties. They wanted correspondents to use the words low or light when discussing Allied dead and wounded. Having their stories cut to pieces by censors discouraged many reporters. Some simply gave up, returning to their newspapers or wire-service bureaus to work as editors.

On August 6, 1945, a U.S. B-29 nicknamed the *Enola Gay* dropped an atomic bomb on the city of Hiroshima, Japan. That single bomb destroyed a 4-square-mile (10-square-kilometer) area at the center of the city. More than eighty thousand civilians died. Three days later, a second atomic bomb was dropped on the city of Nagasaki.

The United States received a message from the Japanese accepting Allied peace terms on August 14, 1945. The surrender agreement was officially signed on September 2. World War II was over.

After the war, General MacArthur took over as supreme commander of Allied occupation forces in Japan. MacArthur made censorship regulations even tighter. He placed all of southern Japan off-limits to the press.

No U.S. reporter had yet been to Hiroshima or Nagasaki to report on the effects of the atomic blasts. MacArthur's ban of visits meant that correspondents and broadcasters would have to be satisfied with official accounts of the bombings.

But Wilfred Burchett of the *London Daily Express* managed to get to Hiroshima by train. He spent the morning of September 3 surveying what was left of the city. His story appeared in the *Daily Express* two days later. It contained disturbing information.

> In Hiroshima, thirty days after the first atom bomb destroyed the city and shook the world, people are still dying, mysteriously and horribly, people who were

uninjured in the cataclysm—from an unknown something which I can only describe as the atomic plague. Hiroshima does not look like a bombed city. It looks as if a monster steamroller had passed over it and squashed it out of existence. I write these facts as dispassionately as I can in the hope that they will act as a warning to the world.

The "atomic plague," as Burchett termed it, was radiation sickness. U.S. authorities denied there was any such thing. They accused

A soldier views the devastation of the atomic bomb on Hiroshima, Japan, in 1945.

Burchett of "falling victim to Japanese propaganda." Major General Leslie Groves, who headed the team that developed the bomb, declared, "The talk about radio-activity is so much nonsense."

In the months that followed, millions of words were said and written about the bombing of the two Japanese cities. Articles reported how the bomb came to be built. They reported how the decision was reached to drop it. They debated whether it should have been dropped at all. But William Shawn, managing editor of the *New Yorker*, realized that reporters and broadcasters had ignored what had actually happened to Hiroshima itself. He felt certain there was a story there.

In March 1946, Shawn got in touch with thirty-two-year-old John Hersey, a correspondent who had covered the war in Europe and the Pacific. Hersey's work had been widely praised. At the outset, Hersey felt unsure how to handle the topic. "The problem of how to deal with such a massive event was very, very...difficult to figure out," Hersey told an interviewer for the Smithsonian Institution.

After visiting Hiroshima and interviewing some twenty-five to thirty survivors, Hersey hit upon a format. He would tell the story of what happened through the eyes of six people who had been at Hiroshima on August 6, 1945. He would tell all that they had seen and felt. He would describe their suffering. The *New Yorker* gave over its entire

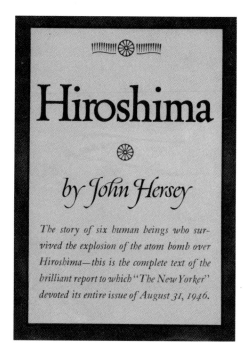

John Hersey's long article about the bombing of Hiroshima became a best-selling book in 1946.

issue of August 31, 1946, to Hersey's article. It was written in a calm, straightforward, and restrained manner.

The article created a sensation. The magazine sold out immediately on newsstands. Bootleg copies sold for fifteen and twenty dollars. Requests for reprints flooded into the *New Yorker*. It was quickly published in book form as *Hiroshima*. More than three million copies have been sold. It remains in print to this day.

For the United States and its Allies, World War II was a war for survival. To lose the war would have been unthinkable. Correspondents and editors supported the war. They did not criticize the military. They often acted as cheerleaders.

But the role of the war correspondent was soon to change. The conflicts to come would not be world wars; they were to be regional in nature. They lacked the public's wholehearted support. The media would become uneasy with the military, questioning tactics and motives. Unlike World War II, little cheerleading would take place.

It was commonplace for correspondents . . . [to go] out on patrol. We felt it was the only honest way of covering the war.

—Marguerite Higgins, war correspondent, 1951

CONFLICT IN KOREA

In the spring of 1950, Marguerite Higgins got upsetting news. Her bosses at the *New York Herald-Tribune* told her they were planning to transfer her from Berlin, Germany, where she was based at the time, halfway around the world to Tokyo, Japan. There she was to head the *Herald-Tribune*'s Far East bureau. The news was a great disappointment to Higgins. She had been reporting on the intense rivalry between the United States and the Soviet Union and other Communist countries that followed World War II. The rivalry had led to the Cold War (1945–1991) between the two nations.

Higgins's stories about the Cold War often landed on the front page of the *Herald-Tribune*. She believed that Tokyo would be too calm for her. No Cold War was being played out there. What was she going to write about? She had no choice, however. Higgins reluctantly packed her bags and boarded a plane for the Japanese capital. But shortly after her arrival, Higgins's doubts about her new assignment and its lack of excitement were erased. Her life became frantic and full of risk.

Higgins in Korea

South Korea, the southern portion of the Korean Peninsula, just a few hundred miles west of Tokyo, was the reason. On June 24, 1950, in an outgrowth of the Cold War, troops of Communist-ruled North Korea, which laid claim to all of Korea, invaded South Korea, crossing the 38th parallel that divided the two countries. (The 38th parallel is one of the imaginary lines that run east and west and parallel to the equator. These lines mark the earth's latitude.)

The United Nations (UN) reacted quickly. On the same day the war began, the UN Security Council demanded an end to the fighting and told the Communists to retreat to the 38th parallel. When North Korea ignored the UN's demand, President Harry Truman moved to support the UN. On June 27, Truman ordered U.S. air and naval forces to South Korea. A few days later, he sent U.S. ground troops into action.

At the same time, at the request of the United States, the Security Council voted to send a military force to aid South Korea. Seventeen nations contributed troops. General Douglas MacArthur, widely hailed as a hero of World War II in the Pacific, was later named to head the UN command.

In Tokyo, Marguerite Higgins wasted no time in making plans to cover the war. A few days after its outbreak, she was aboard an air force transport plane from Tokyo that delivered the first batch of correspondents to Seoul, the South Korean capital.

All was chaos there. In their sweep southward, North Korean troops had reached the outskirts of Seoul. Fearful of being captured or killed, Higgins and the other correspondents fled the city. The headline on Higgins's first story from Korea read: SEOUL'S FALL BY A REPORTER WHO ESCAPED.

South Korean troops were taking flight too, blowing up roads and bridges to halt the enemy advance. "The events provided the most appalling example of panic that I have ever seen," Higgins wrote. Higgins's escape to the south continued. In her sneakers, an oversized army jacket, and baggy pants, Higgins lived like a refugee, crawling through rice paddies and sleeping in foxholes.

Higgins was on the scene when newly arrived U.S. troops faced the enemy assault from the north for the first time. Poorly equipped and without combat experience, the frightened Americans fell back in panic.

Higgins knew she was witnessing an important story and endured the risks. She wrote: "It was routine to hear comments like, 'Just give me a jeep and I know which direction I'll go in. This mama's boy ain't cut out to be no hero.'"

Marguerite Higgins won a Pulitzer Prize for her dispatches from Korea.

Higgins also quoted a young lieutenant, frightened and angry, who asked her, "Are you correspondents telling the people back home the truth? Are you telling them that out of one platoon of twenty men, we have three left? Are you telling them that we have nothing to fight with, and that this is an utterly useless war?"

At the time, there was no censorship in Korea. Correspondents were asked only to observe military secrecy and not to undermine the authority of field officers.

But reporters' stories of "frightened and whipped" U.S. soldiers angered the military. General MacArthur's headquarters in Tokyo accused some reporters of being traitors. They were said to be giving "aid and comfort to the enemy." Two reporters were banned from the battlefront for what they had written.

Higgins and other correspondents protested. "So long as our government requires the backing of an aroused and informed public opinion," wrote Higgins, "it is necessary to tell the hard bruising truth. It is best to tell graphically the moments of desperation and horror endured by an unprepared army, so that the American public will demand that it does not happen again."

Bigart and Higgins

The *New York Herald-Tribune* also assigned Homer Bigart, a foreign correspondent of long experience, to Korea. Much admired and respected, Bigart had won a Pulitzer Prize for his reporting during World War II.

Bigart, who outranked Higgins at the *Herald-Tribune,* believed that Korea was not big enough for both Higgins and himself. He knew that he would be competing with her to get his stories on the *Herald-Tribune's* front page. Bigart ordered Higgins to return to Tokyo or she would be fired. Higgins refused to go. She continued to travel with the troops, describing the conditions they faced and how poorly prepared and equipped they were.

Covering battle areas in Korea for the New York Herald-Tribune, *reporter Homer Bigart often took big risks to get frontline stories.*

Higgins's bosses in New York backed her up, allowing her to remain in Korea. They figured that the competition between Higgins and Bigart would help to produce even better stories. They were right. Both Higgins and Bigart won Pulitzer Prizes for their work as reporters in Korea. Higgins's Pulitzer Prize was the first ever awarded to a woman journalist.

Homer Bigart wasn't Higgins's only problem in Korea, though. Lieutenant General Walton H. Walker, head of U.S. ground forces in Korea, also caused her distress. "This is not the type of war where women ought to be running around the front lines," Walker said. He ordered Higgins to leave Korea. Higgins replied that she was there as a war correspondent, not as a woman. She then went over Walker's head and appealed to General MacArthur. MacArthur overruled Walker's order, allowing Higgins and other women correspondents to remain.

A Huge Setback

The United States kept pouring men and equipment into South Korea. But the North Korean forces continued to drive southward. Then MacArthur made a surprise move that reversed the course of the war. On September 15, 1950, U.S. Marines and other soldiers made an amphibious landing at Inchon on South Korea's northwestern coast. MacArthur's forces soon captured Seoul and had the North Korean army on the run.

MacArthur's troops crossed into North Korea early in October. They continued to drive toward the Yalu River, which marked the border between North Korea and China. The Chinese Communists ordered more than three hundred thousand troops into South Korea to support the North Korean army. The massive Chinese Communist force quickly overpowered MacArthur's troops, driving them back into South Korea. Seoul was soon in Communist hands for the second time.

MacArthur reacted by announcing new rules of censorship. Reporters were not allowed to mention the low morale of UN troops. And when UN soldiers pulled back in the face of the Chinese Communist onslaught from the north, reporters were not permitted to use the word *retreat* to describe what had happened. The military preferred the word *withdrawal*. That seemed to imply that the pullback was planned and not a wild flight.

Reporters whose stories could embarrass UN forces could be expelled from Korea. In extreme cases, a reporter could be tried before a military court.

The UN command headquarters issued reports on battles and enemy casualties for journalists. British reporters called such briefings fairy tales.

Early in 1951, North and South Korean forces faced one another across the 38th parallel. They were at the same point where they had started six months before.

Television and Korea

At the beginning of the conflict in Korea, Americans relied on both newspapers and radio for war news. Newspapers furnished detailed reports and analysis of the war. Radio contributed up-to-the minute news. Television, introduced to the general public after World War II, also began to play a role.

When the Korean War erupted, only about six million TV sets were in use in the United States. But the demand was enormous. By 1960 the number of sets in use had climbed to sixty million.

While the television networks made an effort to cover the Korean War, doing so was not easy. Television cameras were bulky and heavy and difficult to work with, even under ideal conditions.

News programs in Korea were made on black-and-white film. (Regular color television broadcasts and videotaping both began in the mid-1950s.) It took time to develop the film. To deliver it required more time. Film footage shot in Korea traveled by propeller-driven planes to network headquarters in New York. By the time the film was ready to be broadcast, as much as a week might have passed.

With that kind of time lag, television could not compete with radio or even newspapers when it came to fast-breaking news stories. Where television did excel was in documentaries. These factual and drama-tized reports gave viewers real insight into what the war was like.

Edward R. Murrow, who had won legendary fame for his radio broadcasts from London during the early stages of World War II, was broadcasting a series of radio programs in 1947 titled *Hear It Now*. He traveled to Korea to report major events and interview soldiers caught up in the conflict. In 1951 Murrow converted *Hear It Now* to television. It became *See It Now*.

The See It Now *television documentaries by Edward R. Murrow* (front left) *helped to bring scenes of the Korean War into U.S. living rooms.*

At Christmastime that year, a *See It Now* camera crew showed soldiers at war in Korea. They were pictured hauling heavy equipment, plodding through the mud, struggling to keep warm, and preparing for battle. Everywhere there were scenes of death and destruction. Each of the soldiers pictured identified himself and gave his home address. Murrow both produced and narrated the program. Toward the end, he was pictured on the screen to announce that in the brief time since the scenes were shot, half of the soldiers pictured had been killed, wounded, or reported missing in action.

For Christmas 1952, Murrow went back to Korea. He again told the story of the war by interviewing the people involved in it, including soldiers at the front lines and the wounded in hospitals. Murrow ended the program by saying, "There is no conclusion to this report from Korea because there is no end to the war."

The television critic for the *New Yorker* called the program "one of the most impressive presentations in television's short life." The *New York Daily News* said the documentary provided "the most graphic and yet sensitive pictures of war we have ever seen."

"In Korea," said former newscaster Edward Wakin, "television began learning how to cover a war." Korea was a training ground for American television. The knowledge and experience gained would be put to use with great effect in America's future wars.

Peace Arrives

Although Korean truce talks began in the summer of 1951, bitter fighting continued for another two years. Once peace negotiations began, tough censorship rules were put in place. Reporters were not allowed to talk to those conducting the peace talks. Correspondents were forced to rely on daily UN briefings for information.

The war did not end until July 27, 1953, when an armistice agreement was finally signed. Since then, a tough-minded Communist regime has kept tight control in North Korea. Even the ending of the Cold War in

The "talk" graves in this 1952 cartoon stand for the number of lives being lost in the Korean War as the peace talks dragged on.

1991 did not change the situation. The hostility between North and South Korea continued. The United States sought to avoid a shooting war by assigning tens of thousands of troops to South Korea, where many of them were stationed just south of the 38th parallel.

By the beginning of the twenty-first century, North Korea boasted an army of one million troops and a reserve force of almost five million. It ranked as the world's fourth-largest army.

In January 2002, in his State of the Union address, President George W. Bush took note of North Korea's hostile nature. He grouped North Korea with Iran and Iraq and called the three nations an axis of evil. The president said that the three nations were developing weapons of mass destruction. These included not only nuclear weapons but chemical and biological weapons as well. To the Bush administration, North Korea loomed as a threat to world peace.

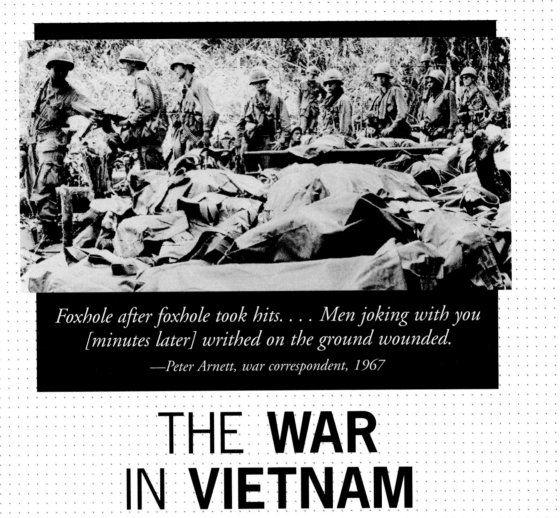

Foxhole after foxhole took hits. . . . Men joking with you [minutes later] writhed on the ground wounded.

—Peter Arnett, war correspondent, 1967

THE **WAR** IN **VIETNAM**

U.S. war correspondents supported the military in World War II. They went along with the nation's military policies in Korea. But the war in Vietnam (1957–1975) was different.

Many military leaders believed that the press and television opposed the war and that this opposition helped to turn the U.S. public against the fighting. U.S. troops were withdrawn from Vietnam as a result, allowing a Communist takeover of the country. To this day, it is widely held in military circles that the media lost the war in Vietnam.

A different opinion was delivered by Colonel Harry G. Summers in testimony before the Senate Governmental Affairs Committee in 1991. Summers said that "blaming the media for the loss of the Vietnam War was wrong. The media, and television in particular, [were] good at showing the cost of the war. But [the] cost of anything has meaning only in relation to value. It was not the news media, which reported the price, that lost the war. It was the government which . . . failed to establish its value."

America's involvement in the Vietnam War had its roots in U.S. foreign policy, which sought to prevent the expansion of Communism. Three U.S. presidents—Dwight D. Eisenhower, John F. Kennedy, and Lyndon B. Johnson—did what they thought was necessary to prevent the collapse of South Vietnam and establish a non-Communist state there.

North vs. South

The conflict in Vietnam went through several stages. Beginning in 1946, the French, who had colonized the region in the mid-1800s, fought the Vietnamese for control of the nation. The French went down to defeat in 1954. After that, Vietnam was divided into Communist North Vietnam and non-Communist South Vietnam.

By 1958 a fierce civil war was in progress. The South Vietnamese army struggled against Communist-trained Vietnamese rebels. The rebels, known as the Vietcong, received military help from North Vietnam. In time, the Vietcong became a serious threat. By 1963 the government of South Vietnam stood on the brink of collapse. The United States had steadily supported the South Vietnamese by sending them weapons and ammunition. Thousands of military advisers were also sent.

During the late 1950s and early 1960s, the press and television had little interest in what was happening in Vietnam. But as America's role expanded and became more serious, more correspondents and broadcasters began going to Southeast Asia.

The *New York Times* sent twenty-eight-year-old David Halberstam to Vietnam in 1962. At the time, correspondents were permitted to journey almost at will throughout South Vietnam. Often they were able to use military ground transportation or would be invited to travel in army helicopters. Halberstam often took advantage of this policy, traveling about the country, spending time with soldiers. Gradually Halberstam decided that the South Vietnamese troops often acted cowardly in battle. The Vietcong, he believed, on the other hand, fought bravely and well.

Early in January 1963, the first important battle of the war took place at Ap Bac, southwest of Saigon, the capital of South Vietnam. In the battle, the Vietcong, equipped with only light weapons, defeated a much larger South Vietnamese force.

Halberstam reported how South Vietnamese troops would not stand and fight and how three U.S. advisers were killed in attempting to lead the South Vietnamese troops into action. He wrote that South Vietnamese artillery shells had accidentally killed South Vietnamese soldiers.

Halberstam's stories were an irritation to the White

Photographers, such as freelancer Robert Ellison (left, pictured with an unidentified colleague), *and correspondents were free to travel almost anywhere in South Vietnam. This easy access—without military supervision—later earned them criticism from the U.S. military.*

House. President Kennedy sought to have Halberstam removed from the scene. He asked Arthur O. Sulzberger, publisher of the *New York Times,* to give Halberstam another assignment, anything but Vietnam. Sulzberger refused to do so. He also canceled a two-week vacation that Halberstam was about to take. He didn't want it to appear that the *Times* was giving in to pressure from the White House.

Several other correspondents wrote how poorly the war was going for the South Vietnamese and how their troops had displayed little willingness to fight. These correspondents included Malcolm W. Browne of the Associated Press, Neil Sheehan of United Press International, and Charles Mohr of *Time* magazine. Conservative reporters and columnists sharply criticized them, saying they were inexperienced and irresponsible.

Marguerite Higgins of the *New York Herald-Tribune* was also critical of these correspondents. Higgins was in Vietnam during the summer of 1963. Afterward, she wrote that she was unable to understand the attitude of such reporters as Halberstam and Mohr. "Reporters here would like to see us lose the war to prove that they are right," she wrote. Halberstam was upset. He believed that Higgins didn't know the real situation in Vietnam. He accused her of not being skeptical enough of what she was being told by high-ranking military officers. Halberstam and Browne later shared a Pulitzer Prize for their early reports from Vietnam.

The Reporting Expands

After President Kennedy was assassinated on November 22, 1963, Lyndon B. Johnson became president. During his first months in office, Johnson did little to increase America's role in Vietnam. But little by little, Johnson changed the character of the war. In 1965 Johnson ordered the first bombings of North Vietnam. By the end of 1965, 180,000 U.S. troops were in Vietnam. By the end of 1968, nearly 500,000 U.S. soldiers were there.

On a surprise visit to Vietnam in 1966, President Lyndon B. Johnson greeted U.S. troops.

As the military buildup continued, the number of correspondents and broadcasters in Vietnam increased considerably. The war was, after all, the biggest news story in the world at the time. In 1968, according to John Pilger, author of *Heroes,* 649 journalists were accredited to the Saigon press corps. Getting accredited was not difficult. Applying for an entry visa from the South Vietnamese was the first step. Once the visa was granted, the next step was to show up in Saigon. The correspondent-to-be had to present U.S. military authorities with a letter from a newspaper requesting accreditation. If the reporter was a freelance writer, two letters were needed from publications that had agreed to buy the articles.

Some correspondents worked for the big news organizations, the Associated Press or United Press International. Others worked for well-known newspapers or the television networks. And hundreds of others represented small-town newspapers, college newspapers, or religious publications. Such publications as *Mademoiselle, True Adventure,* and the *Lithuanian Worker* also had correspondents in Vietnam.

Censorship was not a big problem. Instead, an honor system was used. Correspondents agreed not to disclose certain kinds of information, such as the number of casualties or troop movements. But dispatches did not have to be cleared by military authorities. Correspondents sent what they wrote.

Journalists respected this policy. As Wallace Terry, who covered the Vietnam War for *Time* magazine, once recalled, "I always cooperated with the military in terms of any embargoes or any way they wanted to protect their exercises because I looked at every soldier who was fighting as my fellow citizen . . . and not as a possible scoop."

Instead of censoring news reports, the military sought to promote its version of the war by means of a public relations campaign. Correspondents were invited to attend military press briefings held each afternoon at the Joint United States Public Affairs Office in Saigon. These were meant to provide journalists with hard news stories. But the briefings were often based on inaccurate reports and were overly optimistic. Most correspondents did not take them seriously. The briefings were called the "five o'clock follies" because they provided no solid information.

Women in Vietnam

Many women correspondents were stationed in Vietnam—in record numbers, in fact. According to military records, some three hundred women were approved to cover the war between 1965 and 1975. (Between 1951 and 1975, a total of about two thousand correspondents were accredited to cover the war in Vietnam.)

The military provided what Gloria Emerson, a correspondent for the *New York Times*, called easy access to combat operations. She wrote, "We could fly on bombing missions, parachute into hostile territory with an airborne unit, spend a week with the Special Forces

War correspondent Jurate Kazickas (**far left**) *comforts a wounded U.S. Marine hit by enemy fire near the South Vietnamese village of Con Thien.*

in the jungle, hitch a ride on a chopper and land amid rocket and artillery as a battle raged, or be taken prisoner like a soldier. This access gave women reporters a chance to show that they could cover combat bravely and honorably, holding their own under the most frightening and stressful circumstances."

Jurate Kazickas, a twenty-four-year-old researcher for *Look* magazine, longed for the chance to go to Vietnam as a correspondent. Her boss told her that the magazine would not send her there. Kazickas managed to land a spot as a contestant on the television game show *Password.* She won five hundred dollars and used the prize money to buy a one-way ticket to Saigon.

Once accredited, she preferred doing combat reporting. This involved trudging through jungles and slogging through swamps with U.S. troops. It also involved occasionally dodging mortar fire.

Some commanding officers didn't like the idea that she often visited battle sites. They asked her why she wasn't writing about orphans or refugees. She said, "If I heard it once, I heard it a thousand times. 'Combat is no place for a woman.'"

One day, Kazickas was interviewing a group of marines at Khe Sanh, a combat post that had been besieged by the North Vietnamese. Suddenly she heard a whistling sound and someone shouting, "Incoming!" Instead of throwing herself on the ground as the marines did, Kazickas ran for a bunker. When the rocket exploded, shrapnel tore into Kazickas's face, arms, legs, and buttocks. She spent weeks recovering in a hospital in Da Nang. One colonel remarked, sarcastically, "Well, she got what she was looking for."

As this suggests, leaving Saigon and venturing into the field could be very dangerous. The sad truth is that forty-five correspondents were killed in Vietnam. Many died in helicopter crashes or from stepping on land mines.

Vietnam on TV

As the war in Vietnam kept getting bigger and bigger, television's role in reporting the war steadily became more and more important. Newspapers lost their commanding position. Not only had TV gotten bigger,

During the Vietnam War, CBS anchor Walter Cronkite (at rear, with microphone) *made several trips to South Vietnam to film reports for his nightly news telecast.*

it had gotten better. By the mid-1960s, advances in production technology had greatly improved the quality of TV's news programs. The visual images had become more vivid, more immediate. By this time, most networks were offering their programs in full color.

Nevertheless, television seldom offered scenes of real combat. Thanks to videotaping, which was introduced in the 1950s, there was no long developing process, as with film. Videotapes could be played back immediately. Flown by jet aircraft from Saigon to New York, tapes could sometimes be broadcast on the same day they were shot.

The *New Yorker*'s Michael Arlen described what appeared on home screens, " . . . scenes of helicopters, tall grasses blowing in the helicopter wind, American soldiers fanning out across a hillside on foot, rifles at the ready, with now and then [on the sound track] a far-off ping or two, and now and then [as the grand visual finale] a column of dark billowing smoke a half a mile away invariably described as a burning Vietcong ammo dump."

Some exceptions to television's brief and often inoffensive coverage came to light. For example, Morely Safer of CBS went with a marine search-and-destroy mission to the village of Cam Re, not far from Da Nang. The marines used matches, flamethrowers, and their Zippo lighters to destroy the villagers' thatched huts. The marines tried to tell the villagers to flee, but they would not. Safer finally asked that his Vietnamese cameramen be allowed to speak to the village's older men and women.

Safer's report concluded with these words: "The day's operation burned down 150 houses, wounded three women, killed one baby, wounded one Marine, and netted four old men who could not answer questions in English. . . . There is little doubt that American firepower can win a military victory here. But to a Vietnamese peasant whose home means a life of backbreaking labor it will take more than presidential promises to convince him that we are on his side."

Such reports were rare. Nevertheless television had great impact. Its daily war coverage fueled the debate between the hawks, those who favored the war, and the doves, those who opposed it. Television provided information for both viewpoints.

"In general," said Professor Lawrence Lichty, "for two years after the U.S. troop buildup in 1965, network television reporting overall was favorable to the U.S. effort in Vietnam." A survey conducted by *Newsweek* in 1967 supported this idea. Those surveyed were asked whether television coverage had made them feel like backing the troops or opposing the war. Some 64 percent said they were inclined to support the soldiers. Only 26 percent opposed the war. Tet changed everything.

The Tet Offensive

Tet is the name given to the first day of the Vietnamese New Year. In the early morning hours of January 31, 1968, which was the Tet holiday that year, the Vietcong launched fierce attacks on all of South Vietnam's major cities and many military installations.

U.S. Marines run through the streets of Hue, South Vietnam, during the 1968 Tet Offensive.

U.S. forces were caught by surprise. Savage fighting resulted. Hue, the former Vietnamese capital, fell to the Communists. The guerrillas even attacked the U.S. embassy in Saigon.

In terms of military strategy, the Tet attack failed. The U.S. and South Vietnamese forces ousted the enemy from the positions it had seized. And the Vietcong suffered tremendous losses. But Tet shocked Americans. The nation's leaders had reported important military gains only a short time before. They had been very positive about events in Vietnam. The American people wondered how the enemy could undertake such a high-powered offensive.

Victory in Vietnam seemed to be a long way off. Americans began to seriously question whether halting Communist expansion in Southeast Asia was worth the great costs in lives and money. Leading newspapers and magazines began to declare their opposition to the war. They called for de-escalation—a shrinking of America's role. They called for troop withdrawals. The public's opposition to the war became more widespread. President Johnson responded by reducing the amount of bombing in Vietnam and calling for peace negotiations. And Johnson stunned Americans with the announcement that he did not intend to be a candidate in the 1968 presidential election. Peace talks began in May 1968. They inched along, producing no agreement.

Richard M. Nixon was elected president in November 1968, winning in a landslide over George McGovern, a peace-at-any-price candidate. Nixon knew that he had to reverse U.S. policy in Vietnam. He called for the withdrawal of U.S. forces. Troops began leaving in July 1969.

Antiwar feeling deepened further when *Newsweek* and *Time* carried major stories late in 1969 about a U.S. Army unit that had massacred more than one hundred men, women, and children in the remote village of My Lai. The horror of My Lai led even more Americans to question the nation's objectives in Vietnam.

By this time, the Vietnam War had become the longest war in U.S. history. Following My Lai and the withdrawal of some U.S.

troops, newspapers and television began to lose interest in the war. In 1968, 637 correspondents were in Vietnam. By 1970 the number had dropped to 392, and in 1972 to 295.

Later in 1972, when peace negotiations bogged down, Nixon ordered an all-out bombing of Hanoi, the capital of North Vietnam. Peace talks resumed. Finally, on January 27, 1973, a cease-fire agreement was signed. The last U.S. troops left Vietnam in March 1973. All but a few reporters went with them. The cease-fire agreement did not last long. By late 1974, North Vietnamese troops were on the attack against a now weakened South Vietnam.

The end for South Vietnam came quickly. Saigon was in Communist hands by the end of April 1975. U.S. Marines helped evacuate the last Americans from the U.S. embassy by helicopter. Meanwhile, other journalists, such as Dith Pran and Sydney Schanberg, were reporting on the conflicts that had erupted in neighboring Cambodia as an outgrowth of the Vietnam War.

"Peace with Honor"

The Vietnam War was the first in U.S. history in which a U.S. combat force failed to achieve its goals. Some in the military felt humiliated by the Vietnam experience. Others were bitter.

To some, the media—television, in particular—were to blame for what had happened. Night after night, TV news programs made Americans see and feel what was happening in Vietnam. And when students, members of the clergy, and even newly returned Vietnam veterans began demonstrating against the war, television cameras were there to record their protests.

Some U.S. military leaders believed that the press and television reporters had been given too much freedom in covering the war in Vietnam. Journalists were uncensored. They could go wherever they wanted and talk to anyone they wanted. Military leaders were determined to change that policy.

*Residents emerged . . .
to wave Kuwaiti flags.
. . . I realized . . . this
was the liberation of
Kuwait City.*
—Edward Barnes, the
first reporter in liberated
Kuwait, 1991

GRENADA AND OPERATION DESERT STORM

After Vietnam, U.S. military leaders had bitter feelings toward the press and television. They believed that the media, with its opposition to the war, had turned the public against the conflict. If it had not been for the media, many military leaders believed, the United States could have won the Vietnam War.

The military had a solution. It decided that the press and television had been given too much freedom in Vietnam. They had written and broadcast whatever they wanted, virtually without censorship. The military changed the rules. When U.S. forces invaded the tiny Caribbean island of Grenada in October 1983, the U.S. military tried out a new strategy for dealing with the press and television.

Restoring Order in Grenada

U.S. military action in Grenada was triggered when rebels overthrew the government earlier in 1983. The rebels set up a new government, which established close ties with Cuba, another Caribbean nation, ruled by Communist dictator Fidel Castro.

Other Caribbean nations became fearful of Grenada. They worried that Cuba and even the Soviet Union might use Grenada as a base to support terrorism in Latin America. Several Caribbean nations wanted the United States to help in restoring a democratic form of government to Grenada.

U.S. troops invaded Grenada on October 25, 1983. The action was called for, said President Ronald Reagan, to protect the lives of Americans in Grenada. Troops from six Caribbean nations took part in the operation. Within a matter of days, the U.S. military was in complete control of the island. An elected government was restored to Grenada in 1984.

What was unusual about the invasion was that it took place in total secrecy. The press and television were never informed. Forty-eight hours went by before news of the invasion was made public. Reporters who sought to cover the invasion were not even permitted to go to Grenada. They were kept on a military base on Barbados, an island nation about 125 miles (200 kilometers) to the north and east of Grenada. When the military finally decided to allow reporters to visit Grenada, they limited the number. About three hundred correspondents wanted to cover what was taking place. The military allowed only fifteen reporters and photographers to make the trip.

Once in Grenada, the correspondents were not free to go where they wanted. Military officers took them to sites that had been selected for them. A few correspondents attempted to evade the regulations. They hired a speedboat and tried to reach Grenada on their own. A U.S. fighter plane fired on the boat and forced it to turn back. Later, one of the correspondents who had been aboard the speedboat spoke to Vice Admiral Joseph Metcalf, field commander on the ground in Grenada, about the incident. "Admiral," he asked, "what would have happened if we hadn't turned around?" "We would have blown you right out of the water," the admiral said.

Reporters and broadcasters were furious over the way in which they were treated as they sought to cover the war in Grenada. In response to the protests, the military created a pool system for covering future operations. For interviews or reporting within combat areas, a limited number of correspondents would be chosen from the hundreds that had been accredited. Army officers would escort this small group of correspondents—the pool—to all interviews or military operations. Reporters who were members of a pool would be expected to share their information with non-pool reporters.

The War in the Gulf

The military liked the pool system. It limited the number of reporters with whom they had to deal. It allowed the military to tightly control the flow of information from the war zone. The military decided to rely on pool journalism in future conflicts. The Persian Gulf War gave the military a chance to test their new policy.

The conflict had its beginnings on August 2, 1990, when Iraq invaded its neighbor, the tiny oil-rich nation of Kuwait. After gaining control in Kuwait, Iraq massed huge numbers of troops at Kuwait's border with Saudi Arabia.

The United States and most industrialized nations of the world were fearful. They believed a great disaster loomed if Iraq invaded Saudi Arabia and gained control of the vast oil resources in the region.

President George H. W. Bush moved swiftly. Working with the United Nations, Bush helped to form an international coalition of nations that condemned Iraq's action. The coalition sent troops to Saudi Arabia to protect the nation from possible attack. By mid-October 1990, a total of 450,000 U.S. troops were in Saudi Arabia and other Persian Gulf nations.

The United Nations and coalition nations pressured Saddam Hussein, then Iraq's leader, to withdraw Iraqi forces from Kuwait. But he would not. On January 17, 1991, air strikes on Iraq began. That night, when American families turned on CNN's nightly news

U.S. troops make their way across the Saudi Arabian desert in November 1990 in preparation for the first Persian Gulf War.

broadcast, they saw Iraq's capital city of Baghdad lit up by antiair-craft fire and exploding bombs dropped by U.S. airplanes. It was not film. It was not tape. Thanks to satellites and computers, the video images were live. In late February, coalition forces launched a massive ground attack into Iraq and Kuwait. Television showed that too.

The speed of reporting events underwent tremendous change. Television's live reports from Baghdad were only one of the advances. Reporters in the field were able to send their stories and photographs instantly by means of laptop computers. Portable videophones were another advance. At this stage, however, videophones were often unreliable.

About fourteen hundred reporters and broadcasters were sent to the Gulf region to cover the war. The journalists soon learned that their coverage was to be limited to briefings—that is, daily meetings—with military spokespeople and the media. Only two hundred reporters and broadcasters were selected as pool members.

Following rules set down by the military, members of a press pool were to choose one reporter who would be taken to each newsworthy event by a military escort. After viewing the event, the reporter was to return to share the information that he or she had learned with the other members of the pool. The pool members would then write their versions of the story. A censor had to approve each reporter's story before it could be sent back to the United States.

The pool system was effective in keeping reporters away from the real action. However, in the early stages of the conflict, there was little for reporters to see. It was an air war. Most of the shooting took place in the skies over Iraq. Reporters had no way of covering such action. They found themselves watching planes take off from air bases or missiles being launched from ships in the Persian Gulf.

The daily briefings were a frequent cause for complaint. At these, the military often showed videos of smart bombs. These were bombs that were said to be delivered with pinpoint accuracy. A smart bomb would be shown plunging down a building's ventilator shaft, for instance. Such videos gave the briefings a *Star Wars* flavor. Little solid information about the war was revealed. Reporters would be given detailed counts as to how many tanks or artillery pieces had been destroyed. But how many Iraqi soldiers or civilians had been killed? Journalists were not told.

Sometimes information was purposely withheld from the media. For example, journalists never realized that smart bombs saw only limited use. After the war, General Merril McPeak of the U.S. Air Force said that smart bombs represented only 7 percent of the bombs dropped on Iraq. The others were old-fashioned "dumb" bombs. These included cluster bombs that spread devastation over a wide area.

Briefings sometimes resulted in misinformation being given to the media. Early in the conflict, the Iraqis pumped oil into the Persian Gulf in an effort to prevent coalition amphibious forces from landing in Kuwait. The oil spill story was big news around the world. The British government called Saddam Hussein an environmental terrorist for what he had done. A picture of a dying seabird, a cormorant, coated with oil, was sent out with the story. It was later learned that the poor cormorant was not the victim of something the Iraqis did. The oil that drenched the bird came from another spill, one caused by an American bombing attack.

An oil spill that drenched wildlife was big news during the first Persian Gulf War.

Pool Busting

Some journalists decided that they did not want to be a part of the pool system nor did they want to attend the daily briefings. They decided to strike out on their own. Carl Nolte, a reporter from the *San Francisco Chronicle*, was one of the pool busters. He drove northward from Riyadh, the capital of Saudi Arabia. As *Time* magazine reported, Nolte got lost several times on poorly marked roads. Eventually, however, he came upon a unit of U.S. troops. With no censor to restrain him, Nolte began interviewing. He was able to send out news stories about the soldiers' lack of supplies and paychecks that hadn't arrived.

The military tried to discourage pool busting. More than twenty journalists who tried to evade the military's rules were seized, taken into custody, and threatened with confinement. Some had to endure rough treatment, according to Philip Knightley. Wesley Bocxe, a photographer for *Time* magazine, was blindfolded, searched, and detained for more than thirty hours.

What happened to Bob Simon, a correspondent for CBS, and his three-man crew was much worse. Iraqi forces captured Simon and his crew near the Saudi-Kuwaiti border soon after the Gulf War began. They spent forty days in Iraqi prisons, where they were beaten. For

An early digital image captures the moment when CBS correspondent Bob Simon (center) is freed. He and three colleagues were held in an Iraqi prison for forty days during the first Persian Gulf War.

most of the time, they were held in solitary confinement as suspected spies. "What I did was a stupid mistake," Simon later said in an interview with the *New York Times.* "It's not like we were after some fantastic story and got unlucky. We were just careless."

While the military was able to control most print journalists, a trio of CNN television correspondents managed to report the early stages of the war with relative freedom. The Iraqi government had granted CNN permission for the telecasts. Peter Arnett, Bernard Shaw, and John Holliman, broadcasting from Baghdad, transmitted television images via satellite, keeping many millions of viewers around the world glued to their TV screens.

With satellite technology, viewers could see events as they actually happened. Presented on a round-the-clock basis, the broadcasts depicted the fiery exhaust fumes of missiles in the night skies and sudden illuminations caused by explosions. The sound track was alive with the thunderclap of missiles bursting and the crack of antiaircraft fire.

Arnett credited Holliman with playing a key role in the coverage. "When the bombing started at 2:30 A.M., our communications went down like everyone else's," Arnett recalled in an interview. "We presumed we had been bombed out of existence. But John fiddled with the equipment and ultimately replaced the battery so we could go on with the report. . . ." In the days that followed the first bombing attack, Arnett, Shaw, and Holliman continued their reports via CNN. They came to be known as the Boys of Baghdad.

Arnett, who had won a Pulitzer Prize for his reporting from Vietnam during the war, was later criticized by conservative columnists and broadcasters for what he had transmitted from Baghdad. The Iraqis heavily censored his telecasts, and he was permitted to see only what the Iraqis wanted him to see.

As American viewers were watching Arnett's telecasts, so was the rest of the world. The Iraqis, it was said, were using his reports for propaganda purposes. For example, Arnett reported the Allied bombs had hit a plant that was said to manufacture infant formula. U.S. military officials insisted that it produced biological weapons. It was also feared that Arnett might inadvertently give out information that could be putting coalition troops in danger by reporting the location of military units.

Early in February 1991, twenty-one members of the House of Representatives signed a letter to CNN that claimed that Arnett's dispatches gave Saddam Hussein "a propaganda mouthpiece to over one hundred nations." The broadcasts endangered the lives of "our service personnel," said the letter. Congress urged CNN to "review its current policies on airing the voice of Baghdad."

Senator Alan Cranston of California accused Arnett of being biased in favor of the Iraqis. He said that Arnett was an Iraqi sympathizer. In an interview with journalist Bob Frost, Arnett defended his coverage of the war. He said that he did not think he had "an obligation to get on the team" and help win the war. "To launch a war," said Arnett, "is a political decision by politicians, and the U.S. Constitution doesn't ask the media to back up political decisions, whether they're to go to war or to have a new health scheme or raise taxes. . . . I happen to believe the nation can survive and wars can proceed with the press having freedom to comment and report on what is going on. I'm convinced that it strengthens the national hand rather than weakens it."

CNN's telecasts from Baghdad sent the network's ratings skyrocketing. They also helped to establish CNN as a significant force in the media world. The Baghdad telecasts had one other lasting effect. They persuaded CNN and other networks to cover some events on a wall-to-wall, or continuous, basis. Some call this the mediathon approach.

The War Winds Down

The first Persian Gulf War did not last long. It took only one hundred hours for the United States and coalition troops to defeat the

Iraqi army. President George H. W. Bush declared the war ended on February 27, 1991. A cease-fire agreement was signed on April 6. Kuwait was liberated. But Saddam Hussein was allowed to remain in power in Iraq.

For the American press and television, it was a most unsatisfactory experience. Only a small number of correspondents were permitted access to the battle zones.

The strict limits on news gathering prevented the public from being fully informed about the war. The media's First Amendment rights had been seriously tampered with. A disturbing pattern for future wars had been established.

I made my peace with the fact that at any moment I could die, and I just decided to focus on my job.
—Bernard Shaw, war correspondent, 2003

THE **WAR** ON **TERRORISM**

On September 11, 2001, terrorists slammed jetliners into the twin towers of New York's World Trade Center and a third hijacked airliner crashed into the Pentagon outside Washington, D.C. A new chapter began in U.S. history. Both towers collapsed that day, bringing the death toll to almost three thousand people. A fourth hijacked jet crashed into a field in Pennsylvania. "We're at war," President George W. Bush declared a few days after the attacks. "There's been an act of war declared upon America by terrorists, and we will respond accordingly."

No one doubted the president's words. With the attacks of September 11, the United States launched a war on terrorism. The conflict was unlike any other war in the nation's history. There was no nation to be conquered. The war had no clearly defined battle zones; it was global.

And no one had any idea how long the war was going to last. President Bush said only that it was to be a lengthy war. That judgment was not disputed. Some worried that the war on terrorism would be like the war on drugs or the war on crime. It would be a war without end.

Soon after September 11, the U.S. government named members of a worldwide terrorist network known as Al-Qaeda as those responsible for the attacks. Al-Qaeda is headed by Osama bin Laden, a wealthy Saudi Arabian and an extremist of Islam, the religion followed by the world's more than one billion Muslims.

In 1998 bin Laden and his supporters had declared a jihad, or holy war, against Christians and crusaders. Al-Qaeda had found a place of safety in Afghanistan, a country in southwestern Asia about the size of Texas. To the nation's west lies Iran. Pakistan is to the east and south.

Attacking the Taliban

In Afghanistan bin Laden allied himself with the Taliban, an Islamic fundamentalist faction. By 1998 the Taliban had gained control of 90 percent of Afghanistan.

Like fundamentalists of other religions, the Taliban believed in the very strict observance of their religion's laws. They rejected modern Islam. They believed it to be too permissive.

Under the Taliban, strict rules of dress and behavior were enforced. Television, the Internet, movies, nonreligious music, and dancing were banned. Women were harshly treated. The Taliban demanded that every woman wear a burka, a shroudlike garment that covered the body from head to toe. Women could not work or attend school.

The Taliban and bin Laden proved to be a well-matched pair. Bin Laden supplied money and manpower to support the Taliban. In return, the Taliban allowed bin Laden to set up terrorist training camps in Afghanistan.

With bin Laden in Afghanistan rejoicing over the success of his murderous mission on September 11, President Bush set to work to build an international coalition to respond to the attacks. Great Britain offered the strongest support. Russia said it would work with the alliance. Japan promised military help. Pakistan and other nations agreed to allow U.S. aircraft to use their bases.

President Bush and his military advisers also won the support of the Northern Alliance, a faction within Afghanistan that had been actively opposing the Taliban. Northern Alliance fighters controlled about 5 percent of the country. They were to play an important role in combating the Taliban.

Late in September 2001, the U.S. military alerted forty journalists from seventeen news organizations—including the *New York Times,* the *Washington Post,* and the *Wall Street Journal*—to be ready to relocate. They were flown to the Middle East and assigned to aircraft carriers that were operating in the Arabian Sea off the coast of Pakistan. The journalists realized that an attack was at hand. But they withheld what they knew. They did not want to endanger the lives of the troops or put the operation itself in jeopardy.

On October 7, America's war on terror began in earnest. Cruise missiles struck at Taliban and al-Qaeda defenses in Afghanistan. MSNBC, a cable network, broke the news of the air raids in the United States. Soon after, all of the TV networks were running fuzzy images of the attacks.

But coverage was not as sweeping as it had been during the first Gulf War. In that conflict, the Iraqi government allowed CNN to

U.S. Marines arrived in southern Afghanistan in late 2001, after the al-Qaeda attacks of September 11.

broadcast twenty-four hours a day from Baghdad. It was much different in Afghanistan. The Taliban would not permit any U.S. news organizations to enter areas of the country under its control. Because of the Taliban's order, U.S. TV networks had to obtain images from the British Broadcasting Corporation (BBC) and from Al-Jazeera, an Arabic-language TV network.

Besides frequent scenes of U.S. bombing raids, Al-Jazeera also occasionally offered videotaped messages from Osama bin Laden himself. In one, he praised those who had conducted the attacks of September 11. In no other war had Americans been addressed by

After September 11, 2001, the videotaped image of Osama bin Laden appeared frequently on Al-Jazeera, an Arabic-language television network. U.S. networks rebroadcast his appearances.

the face and voice of the enemy. It had a chilling effect upon many viewers at home.

Backpack Journalism

Just as the war against terrorism was unlike any war in U.S. history, efforts by journalists to cover the conflict were different from previous wars. Technology was one of the differences. Reporters who headed out to Afghanistan from the United States were equipped with laptops, cell phones, and videophones. These made possible live transmission from virtually any part of Afghanistan.

The technological mix also included the Internet. "We are reporting for a public that checks back with their favorite Web sites four, five, six times a day," said Tom Kent, a deputy managing editor for the Associated Press. "They expect to see updated news."

The fact that journalists could transmit their stories electronically and in the blink of an eye worried military leaders. In World War II, for example, journalists typed out their stories and handed them to military censors for review. But in Afghanistan, many correspondents carried with them the means of sending back their stories. They could file what they had written from any place at any time. Backpack journalism, as it was called, made U.S. military leaders uneasy. They realized that they had no control over what might be written or broadcast.

The military responded by limiting reporters' access to battle zones. The same tactic had been used in 1990 during Operation Desert Storm. The military found it to be a very effective form of censorship.

War on Journalists

Censorship, however, was not the most serious problem faced by journalists assigned to cover the war in Afghanistan. Keeping alive was. Members of the press were often looked upon as the enemy.

Journalists are "in the bull's-eye out there," said Alex Jones, director of the Joan Shorenstein Center on the Press, Politics, and Public Policy at Harvard University. "If the Taliban gets a hold of you, they're apt to execute you. We shouldn't be naïve. This is a sophisticated, bloodthirsty bunch."

Eight correspondents were killed in Afghanistan during the first year of the U.S. war on terrorism, according to the Committee to Protect Journalists. That total did not include the kidnapping and murder of Daniel Pearl, a reporter for the *Wall Street Journal.* Pearl, thirty-eight years old, was in Karachi, Pakistan, working on a story about a small, actively aggressive Islamic group. Late in January 2002, he was reported missing. Pearl and his wife had been living in

This photograph of Wall Street Journal *reporter Daniel Pearl was taken while being held captive by Pakistani militants early in 2002. He was murdered shortly afterward.*

Karachi. His articles often reported the growing tensions between Pakistan and India. Pearl had been trying to arrange an interview with an Islamic cleric at the time he disappeared.

A few days after Pearl was reported missing, a group calling itself the National Movement for the Restoration of Pakistani Sovereignty claimed responsibility for kidnapping him. The group sent an e-mail to several news organizations in the United States and Pakistan. The e-mail contained four photographs of Pearl. One of them was frightening. It showed Pearl being held with a gun to his head.

The group that captured Pearl accused him of being an agent for the Central Intelligence Agency (CIA). The *Wall Street Journal* was quick to deny the charge. "Mr. Pearl, a U.S. citizen born in the U.S., and a working journalist all his adult life, is not an agent of any government or agency," said a spokesperson for the newspaper. "He is a reporter for us—nothing more, nothing less." Later, Pearl's captors claimed that he worked for Mossad, the Israeli intelligence agency. Reporters who worked with Pearl knew that to be another false accusation. Pearl, they said, was a journalist, nothing more.

In February 2002, U.S. government officials received a videotape that contained a series of horrifying images. In one, Pearl was shown being executed by his captors. Months later, Pearl's body was found in a shallow grave on the outskirts of Karachi.

Pearl's murder sent a message to journalists everywhere. No longer were they going to be looked upon as neutral observers. They would often be regarded as the enemy. They would be targets.

Bob Woodruff, a correspondent for ABC News who was assigned to cover operations in Afghanistan, worked with certain precautions. "You don't travel alone at night," he said. "Watch your back in public places. When it feels unsafe, get out."

Some journalists considered carrying weapons. But most agreed that was not a good idea. Roy Gutman, a correspondent for *Newsday*, based in Washington, D.C., expressed the feelings of many of his colleagues when he said that journalists are "really better off being unarmed. The moment you carry a weapon, you are reasonably suspected of being part of a military organization." Most correspondents agree—a weapon makes a journalist seem to be a participant in the conflict; it increases the danger.

Although ground troops were vital during the war in Afghanistan, the campaign was one that stressed airpower and precision strikes. It was highly successful. In only three months, U.S. forces, along with Afghan help, had overthrown the Taliban and had stripped al-Qaeda of its operations base. A new government was put in place.

U.S. military leaders were confident that the Taliban and al-Qaeda forces in Afghanistan had been sharply reduced. A battle had been won. But the war on terrorism had just begun. As for Osama bin Laden, his exact whereabouts were a mystery. Was he dead or alive? No one could say.

*In this war, you were there living with these guys; . . .
you were in . . . as much danger as they were.*
—*John Roberts, CBS correspondent, 2003*

A FRESH APPROACH

The scene could have been from the war in Afghanistan. An army transport helicopter, its blades whirring and under fire, eases in for a gentle landing on a patch of red earth. Its wheels hardly touch down when a ten-person squad of what appear to be combat troops, helmeted with heavy backpacks, leap out. They crouch in semicircles on both sides of the aircraft. These are not combat troops preparing for

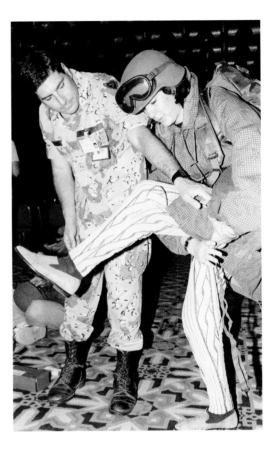

CNN correspondent Christiane Amanpour struggles with straps for a gas mask bag.

battle. They carry no weapons. And this is not Afghanistan. These are potential war correspondents. They are taking part in a training program at the Quantico Marine Corps Base in Virginia. First offered by the U.S. Department of Defense in the fall of 2002, the new program was meant to prepare journalists to operate safely on the battlefield with frontline units.

The weeklong instruction program was called a media boot camp. Journalists got schooled in camouflage, concealment, and land navigation. They were taught to maneuver under fire. They learned the basics of minefield detection and combat first aid. They were trained in how to protect themselves in the event of chemical or biological attack. They learned how to create field latrines. They were even supplied with Marine Corps training manuals.

One manual advised reporters what to do if taken captive and held as a hostage. It suggested that hostages smile, greet their captors by name, and seek to determine common interests. "Fight despair and depression by keeping a positive mental outlook," the text said.

The boot camp was one phase of the U.S. Department of Defense's new policy of granting journalists greater access to the battlefield. Such access was denied during the wars in the Persian Gulf and Afghanistan. Reporters and news organizations protested the restrictions. They were a form of censorship, they said. They were not able to keep the public properly informed as a result. In response to the outcry, the military announced it would change its policy. It would take a new approach in dealing with the media.

In making a change, the military was not merely giving in to the newspapers and broadcasters. Military leaders were being realistic. They realized that control of the news had been slipping away from them. Satellite links had led to an enormous flood of information from battle sites. The Department of Defense pledged that military operations in the next war would be seen close up by journalists. And these journalists would be trained to operate in war zones.

Embedded Media

Under the new approach, reporters, photographers, and television crews were to be placed within—embedded in—individual military units. Embedded journalists would travel with the unit to the battle site. They would go into combat with the unit. A few restrictions were in place, however. Reporters could not reveal a unit's exact location. They would not be permitted to carry or use firearms. Photographers could not use flash photography at night.

Critics said the military had made such promises before but failed to live up to them. Would the military honor its most recent pledge of cooperation? Critics did not have to wait long to find out. Late in January 2003, in his State of the Union address, President George W. Bush warned that the nation of Iraq was helping and protecting terrorists. He said that the United States needed to strike Iraq soon if the nation failed to disarm.

On TV screens across the United States, live images of reporters in Iraq were shown with the sights of war in the background.

While President Bush managed to gain Great Britain as an ally, few other nations offered their support. That didn't seem to bother the president. More and more, he spoke of the need to rid Iraq of Saddam Hussein.

As the nation's war strategy was being developed, military leaders moved ahead with plans to embed press, TV, and radio reporters with combat troops. More than six hundred correspondents would eventually be assigned to military units. Reporters would live, eat, sleep, and move into combat with their assigned unit.

Naturally, such media giants as the *New York Times* and NBC planned to embed reporters. So did a wide range of other news outlets, including *People* magazine, *Rolling Stone, Men's Health,* and MTV. Twenty percent of the correspondents were from the foreign press, including Al-Jazeera.

A good number of journalists from the cable news networks—Fox News, CNN, and MSNBC—would also be traveling with the armed forces. Cable had become the leading source of news, according to a survey conducted in January 2002. Newspapers and local television ranked second and third. Network TV news was fourth (although the major nightly news shows still led in total number of viewers).

U.S. forces massed in the Persian Gulf for the assault. Several aircraft carriers and the air force's most modern fighters and bombers were ready. Foreign troops, including those from Great Britain and Australia, also gathered.

War in Iraq

In March 2003, President Bush issued a final warning to Saddam Hussein, demanding that he leave Iraq within forty-eight hours. When he did not, the war began. As U.S. tanks and armored personnel carriers sped northward through the desert into Iraq from their bases in Kuwait, embedded reporters went with them. Other correspondents filed stories from aircraft carriers and air bases.

From the beginning, reporters filled TV screens with the sights and sounds of war. Interviews with young and determined military personnel produced firsthand accounts of what was taking place. A pilot assigned to the aircraft carrier *Abraham Lincoln* returned to the ship following a mission supporting ground troops. He had to make a difficult landing through thick clouds and swirling sand. A reporter from the *New York Times* was there to record his remarks. "It was crazy, the worst I've ever seen," he said. "My knees were still shaking when I stepped out of the plane."

Sometimes the reports were frank and revealing. A CNN reporter interviewed a young marine private who complained of feeling faint, unable to carry his pack, and of missing his family. "He's just kind of having a hard time right now," a comrade explained.

CNN anchor Aaron Brown praised the coverage as historic. "No matter how you slice the thing," he said, "this is an extraordinary picture of a moment in a war. This is not the kind of thing that has ever happened before." Brown read an e-mail message from the mother of a tank commander, who wrote, "Thank you for allowing me to sit with my son as he crossed the desert into Iraq."

Embedded correspondents reported not only U.S. victories and losses but also the ugly side of the war. At military checkpoints inside Iraq, U.S. troops sometimes shot at civilian vehicles that they thought carried enemy fighters. In one incident, U.S. gunfire wiped out an entire family. Such stories were carried by ABC News and appeared in the *Washington Post.*

David Bloom, an NBC correspondent embedded with a tank convoy, sent some of the war's most vivid pictures into U.S. living rooms. In a helmet and bulletproof vest, with wind-blown hair and a dirt-streaked face, Bloom reported events as his convoy's tanks raced through the desert toward Baghdad.

Bloom operated from an M88 tank recovery vehicle that had been outfitted with a mobile satellite transmitting unit. He could send sharp pictures traveling at speeds of up to 50 miles (80 kilometers) per hour. His camera transmitted microwave signals to a converted Ford truck several miles back in the convoy. From the truck, Bloom's images were beamed to NBC. Bloom was on the air around the clock, reporting in the heat of the desert sun, during fierce sandstorms, and on pitch-black nights, his face eerily illuminated by glow sticks. Tragically, Bloom died while covering the war, not from enemy action but from a blood clot that proved fatal. Bloom was the second U.S. journalist to die in the Iraq war. Michael Kelly, editor at large for the *Atlantic Monthly,* was killed earlier in a vehicle accident.

One of the most tragic incidents occurred when a U.S. tank fired an artillery shell at the Palestine Hotel in Baghdad, where U.S. and foreign correspondents were housed. Three journalists died in the attack. The U.S. military claimed that the tank had fired in self-defense against a sniper in the hotel. Journalists in the building disputed this. Some media sources said the attack may have been a war crime.

Besides the journalists who were embedded with military units, most major news organizations also had correspondents roaming the region. One of these was Geraldo Rivera of Fox News. In covering the war, Rivera violated one of the military's ground rules. He drew a map in the sand before a television camera that revealed the position of a military unit. The next day, military officers demanded that Rivera leave Iraq.

Veteran correspondent Peter Arnett, who had won a Pulitzer Prize for his reporting in Vietnam, was another violator. Working for National Geographic Explorer and NBC, Arnett had been assigned to cover the news from Baghdad by means of a satellite camera in his hotel room.

NBC's Matt Lauer (left) *interviews Peter Arnett following Arnett's dismissal by the network for taking part in a controversial interview on Iraqi television.*

Not long after the United States launched the invasion, Arnett appeared on Iraqi TV to say: "The first [U.S.] war plan has failed because of Iraqi resistance." Arnett also said that reports about civilian casualties had served "to help those who oppose the war" in the United States.

NBC executives decided Arnett had made statements that would aid the Iraqi propaganda machine. The network fired him. So did National Geographic Explorer. Arnett and Rivera were rare cases. Although the war in Iraq was the most heavily covered in history, incidents having to do with media misconduct were few.

The Aftermath

On May 1, speaking from the deck of the aircraft carrier *Abraham Lincoln*, President Bush declared the military phase of ridding Iraq of Saddam Hussein had ended. The nation, the president said, had scored "one victory in a war on terror that began on September 11th, 2001, and still goes on."

With the winding down of military action, news organizations began removing reporters from military units. The idea of embedding journalists with the armed forces in Iraq got positive reviews. The media liked having their reporters with troops in the battlefield. The military liked the flattering coverage the troops received.

In fact, the coverage may have been too flattering. Speaking of the embedded reporters, Marvin Kalb, a noted media watchdog, said: "It served the Bush administration by providing more sympathetic coverage, by being understanding of the soldiers and therefore of that slice of war that each reporter saw. If a reporter were to take a critical tone toward the administration, there were all those other reporters balancing that negative thrust."

Other critics of the war coverage in Iraq said that the military used the media as an instrument of propaganda by embedding reporters with frontline troops. With their folksy interviews from battle zones, reporters helped to shape public opinion in support of the war.

In 2003 President George W. Bush declared the first phase of the war against Iraq to be over. But the war continued.

The Bush administration also presented its version of the war's events through daily briefings for journalists. Staged at the Pentagon in Washington, D.C., the briefings began at seven o'clock in the morning (eastern standard time) so as to be carried by the morning news shows. The briefings continued throughout the day. Cable news programs snapped up the information they supplied.

Officers who conducted the briefings used a language of their own in describing the war's events. For example, at one stage of the war, U.S. and British troops stopped advancing and were said by the press to be bogged down. Briefers avoided that term. It was too negative for them. They described the situation as an operational pause. Briefers also shunned the term civilian deaths, when discussing the killing of nonmilitary Iraqis. That term was too blunt, too harsh. They preferred collateral damage.

The briefers' glossary covered nearly every aspect of the war. Military personnel headed for Iraq received injections of a vaccine to prevent smallpox. Sometimes illnesses developed from the vaccine itself. Three deaths resulted and were described as negative health consequences. During the war, U.S. and British troops were sometimes attacked by members of the fedayeen—fanatic fighters who did not belong to the established Iraqi military forces. The term *fedayeen* means "one who sacrifices himself for a cause." To military briefers, members of the fedayeen were thugs or death squads.

Briefers even had an official name for the war. They called it Operation Iraqi Freedom. This was to underscore President Bush's goal of liberating the Iraqi people from the rule of Saddam Hussein. It was also used to counter the insistence by the war's critics that the United States was chiefly interested in Iraq's oil resources.

The concept of military briefings was not new, of course. Nor was the idea of embedding journalists. In World War II, Ernie Pyle and other journalists traveled with frontline troops.

But the place where a journalist happens to be assigned isn't always critical. It doesn't matter whether he or she is reporting from the battlefront or covering daily briefings at the Pentagon. What is important is the journalist's willingness to challenge the military—to be ready to question how the war is being conducted. This is vital to the public's right to know.

A Second War

The United States and its coalition partners, chiefly Britain and Poland, won the war in Iraq. But winning the peace was another matter.

Despite President Bush's May 2003 declaration that major combat operations had ended in Iraq, resistance soon widened. By the summer of 2003, the United States had become involved in a second conflict, one that proved even more deadly and destructive than the first.

This time the enemy was not an organized military force, and no battle lines existed. The attackers, whom the U.S. military labeled insurgents, were largely extremists of the Sunni branch of Islam. (Islam has two main sects, the Sunnis and the Shiites.) These extremists included members of the Baath Party, which had controlled Iraq during Saddam Hussein's reign, as well as countless foreign terrorists. The insurgents' goal was to drive the United States and other coalition forces out of Iraq and to regain the power they had once held.

Car bombings were the insurgents' favorite method of inflicting slaughter. Sometimes, they'd load vehicles with explosives and set them off from remote locations. More often, suicide drivers would detonate the loaded vehicles upon reaching their target. The insurgents used car bombings to strike coalition checkpoints, security forces, and troop and supply convoys. The worst car bombings produced horrifying results. The extremists also inflicted terror through random shootings, mortar attacks, kidnappings, and beheadings.

U.S.-led coalition troops weren't the insurgents' only targets. The insurgents also launched attacks against foreigners and Iraqi civilians. Iraq's slowly developing police and army, its newly appointed political leaders, and even Islamic aid agencies, such as the Red Crescent, were additional targets. Hundreds of assaults occurred each week.

Journalists, too, found themselves under attack. Much of the country became a no-go zone for them. Journalists who continued to operate developed what was called a bunker mentality. They remained in heavily fortified hotels in Baghdad, leaving the capital for only short periods to travel as embedded correspondents with coalition troops. Even in relatively safe areas of Baghdad, only a handful of correspondents were bold enough to get out of a car, walk around, and attempt to talk to people. "On some days," said one reporter, "it seems we are all crowded into a single room together, clutching our notebooks and watching the walls."

Part of the problem resulted from the way in which the Iraqi people looked upon journalists. Under Saddam Hussein, Iraqi journalists had shown little integrity. Either they were heavily censored, or they wrote what the government wanted them to write. Iraqis thought the U.S. journalists were the same, that is, they were believed to be serving the U.S. government.

The new Iraqi police force was often openly hostile to U.S. journalists. When a photographer from the Knight Ritter newspapers tried to take pictures of a police officer beating a suspect, another

In 2004 a suicide bombing destroyed a hotel used by journalists in Baghdad. More than twenty-five people were killed in the blast.

officer attempted to rip the camera out of her hands. When she refused to give it up, a plainclothes officer came up from behind, drew a gun, pointed it at her, and said he would kill her. Fortunately, an Iraqi government official happened upon the scene and cooled the situation.

U.S. coalition forces did nothing to counteract such frightening incidents. Journalists realized that, unless they happened to be embedded with a military unit, they were on their own.

In January 2005, when millions of Iraqis went to the polls—in what was the nation's first democratic election in decades—journalists had to abide by strict security precautions. TV news organizations, for instance, were barred from filming election officers or polling places. Poll workers were afraid of being identified by anti-American insurgents. Most voters were also off-limits to television. "All of the things we would normally take pictures of to cover this election, we can't take pictures of," said David Wright, a foreign correspondent for ABC News.

Depending on Fixers

Because information gathering by U.S. and European journalists was severely limited, they came to rely more and more on "fixers." These were local journalists who had long worked for foreign correspondents as guides, translators, and interview arrangers. "If you are an Iraqi, you can move around Baghdad more freely," said the news director of an Arab TV channel. "When you have something happening on the ground, a bombing for example, you'll find, more or less, Iraqi and Arab journalists are covering them."

Even in Baghdad, journalists used fixers to gather basic information. According to Mary Braswell, deputy foreign editor of the *Los Angeles Times*, "We might drive to different parts of Baghdad, but were likely to remain in our cars. At times, we've had to send out our translators with a list of interview questions."

In January 2005, the Committee to Protect Journalists (CPJ), declared Iraq to be the deadliest country in the world for journalists. Thirty-six journalists had been killed since the outbreak of hostilities in March 2003. At least twenty others were kidnapped and held for long periods. Most were released, although kidnappers did kill an Italian journalist.

Most Americans were shocked in February 2005, when Eason Jordan, an executive with CNN News, made comments that the U.S. military had actually targeted journalists in Iraq. A storm of outrage followed. The result was that Jordan backtracked, saying he never meant to give the impression that the U.S. military deliberately tried to kill journalists. Despite his change of position, Jordan was forced to resign.

While no evidence existed that U.S. forces intentionally targeted members of the media, U.S. soldiers had unintentionally killed several journalists. No one questioned that insurgents were the leading cause of deaths among journalists in Iraq. But according to Joel Campagna of the CPJ, U.S. military fire is the second cause of death. In February 2005, Campagna said, "At least nine journalists and two media support staff have died as a result of U.S. fire in Iraq in the last 23 months." Campagna called "negligence or indifference" the reason for the deaths. When journalists are killed, said Campagna, "the military often ... seems unwilling to launch an investigation or take steps to mitigate risk."

For the constantly menaced journalists assigned to cover the war in Iraq, the CPJ published an updated edition of its handbook, "On Assignment: A Guide to Reporting in Dangerous Situations." The handbook gave information and advice on helmets and body armor, armored vehicles, first-aid kits, vaccinations, and security training courses. But the committee warned that neither the handbook nor other resources "can ever guarantee safety in any given situation."

"Journalists in dangerous situations must constantly re-evaluate risks and know when to back down," said the handbook. It quoted Terry Anderson, CPJ honorary chairman and a former bureau chief for the Associated Press in Beirut, Lebanon, who said, "Always, constantly, constantly, every minute, weigh the benefits against the risks. And as soon as you become uncomfortable with the equation, get out, go, leave it. It's not worth it. There is no story worth being killed for."

A Reason Why

In March 2005, as the United States entered its third year of military operations in Iraq, journalists there fully realized that they were witnesses to a savage guerrilla war. Neither the newly formed Iraqi government nor U.S. military forces controlled most cities. Car bombings killed and injured scores of people almost on a daily basis. Roads outside of Baghdad were sown with land mines and explosive devices, making the roads unusable. Assassinations, kidnappings, and beheadings continued without letup.

Journalists run to safety during a bombing raid in Baghdad.

Why do journalists remain in Iraq in the face of the unending terrorism and chaos? They stay for the same reasons they risked their lives in Vietnam and Korea, in Europe and the Pacific during World War II, and in all other of the nation's conflicts stretching back a century and a half. It wasn't the big salaries or the opportunities for moving up the career ladder. It wasn't the prestige that often goes with the job. Wars attract the attention of the world, and for many journalists, battle zones are where they want to be. They feel a need and an obligation to tell the story. And many believe what they write can make a difference.

In the Words of Famous Journalists

CHRISTIANE AMANPOUR (born 1958) is the chief international correspondent for CNN. She spent the 1990s hopscotching from one horrific war zone to another. Her assignments took her to Bosnia, Haiti, Algeria, Somalia, Rwanda, Kuwait, and Afghanistan. Here she reports on the condition of women in Afghanistan under the Taliban government. *"The Taliban's adherents have sought to eradicate women from public life. . . . The regime has barred females from taking any job outside the home. . . . Girls have been thrown out of school. . . . Afghan women cannot even expect proper medical care."*

PETER ARNETT (born 1934) became an Associated Press (AP) reporter in 1959. In 1962 AP sent Arnett to Vietnam, where he covered every aspect of the conflict. In 1966 he won a Pulitzer for his writing. He was in Saigon in 1975, as the city was about to be taken over by the North Vietnamese. He sent back this report. *"Those [South Vietnamese] who didn't have a place on the last helicopters out of Saigon—and there were thousands of them left behind—hooted, booed, and scuffled with the Marines guarding the landing zones."*

Arnett joined CNN in 1981, where he became famous as a television foreign correspondent. He covered the Soviet Union during the Gorbachev years and was in Iraq during the first Gulf war. During that war, he interviewed Iraq's then-president Saddam Hussein. He also covered the Iraq war in 2003. At that time, he criticized U.S. policy in an interview with the state-run Iraqi television network, after which CNN fired him.

HOMER BIGART (1907–1991) won two Pulitzer Prizes for his war reporting. One was for his coverage of his flights with the U.S. Air Force during World War II and the other was for the articles he filed from Korea. His Korean accounts sometimes criticized military decision making, as evidenced by this story dated December 5, 1950, when U.S. forces had to retreat in the face of a massive Communist Chinese response.

"To fan out a small force along the rugged fastness of a 700-mile [1,127-kilometer] frontier . . . made no sense. It was an invitation to disaster. . . . A unit commander [noted] that the Chinese Communists had won with virtually no artillery, no armor and no air power. [He said], 'We should avoid fighting in this sort of terrain against an enemy that has a great reserve of manpower.'"

MARGARET BOURKE-WHITE (1904–1971) started taking photographs at a young age. By the time she was twenty-five, she was famous for her artistic photos of industrial machinery. In 1929 Bourke-White hooked up with Henry Luce, who hired her to take pictures for his magazines, first for *Fortune* and later for *Life*. Before and during World War II, she traveled throughout Europe, documenting the soldiers and civilians involved in the conflict. In 1945 she was with General George Patton's troops when they liberated the German death camp at Buchenwald. She described the scene. *"I saw and photographed the piles of naked, lifeless bodies, the human skeletons who would die the next day because they had to wait too long for deliverance. . . . Using the camera was almost a relief. It imposed a slight barrier between myself and the horror in front of me."* Bourke-White went on to photograph Gandhi in India, the effects of apartheid in South Africa, and the guerrilla warfare in Korea, as well as to document many American scenes.

WALTER CRONKITE (born 1916) is best known as the anchor of the *CBS Evening News* from 1962 to 1981. But he started out as a print reporter and covered World War II for United Press International. While at CBS, he traveled to Vietnam several times. He was there during the massive Tet Offensive in 1968. Afterward, he broke with his usual policy of reporting the news without personal commentary, saying, *"It is increasingly clear to this reporter that the only rational way out then will be to negotiate, not as victors, but as an honorable people who lived up to their pledge to defend democracy, and did the best they could."*

RICHARD HARDING DAVIS (1864–1916) was a novelist, short story writer, dramatist, and editor. As a reporter for the *New York Journal*, he became the most influential war correspondent of the Spanish–American War (1898). His dispatches from Cuba helped to create the legend surrounding Theodore Roosevelt and the Rough Riders. Here he gives a moving account of the execution of a young Cuban insurgent. *"He sank on his side in the wet grass without a struggle or a sound, and did not move again. It was difficult to believe that he meant to lie there, that it could be ended without a word, that [he]...would not rise to his feet and continue to walk on over the hills . . . to his home; that there was not a mistake somewhere, or that at least some one would be sorry or say something or run and pick him up."*

GLORIA EMERSON (1929–2004) worked as a correspondent for the *New York Times* in Nigeria, in Northern Ireland, and from 1970 to 1972 in Vietnam. Her articles of human interest and personal experience earned her the George Polk award for excellence in international reporting. Of life in the capital city of Saigon (now Ho Chi

Minh City), she wrote: *"The war had gone into every corner of every life, and the Vietnamese value harmony very much. There was no harmony, there was no order, there was no calm. There was corruption at every possible level, and people were sad and nervous."*

MARTHA GELLHORN (1908–1998) was one of the first journalists to see the Nazi death camp at Dachau. She stayed on to cover the aftermath of World War II Europe and then witnessed battles for independence in Asia and the Middle East. Some of her best reporting—taken up when she was in her seventies—was contained in her accounts of the Vietnam War. Shrewd and experienced, she later said, *"After all this time, I still cannot think calmly about that war. It was the only one I reported on the wrong side."*

FLOYD GIBBONS (1887–1939) was an ambitious and fearless reporter for the *Chicago Tribune*. He was covering World War I before the United States got involved in the conflict. Eager to get an eyewitness story, Gibbons sailed to Europe on a British passenger ship, the *Laconia*. A German submarine torpedoed the vessel without warning. The ship sank, but Gibbons escaped in a lifeboat. His stirring story of the *Laconia*'s last moments appeared in the *Chicago Tribune* on February 26, 1917. Here's an excerpt. *"We rested our oars, with all eyes on the still lighted Laconia. . . . We watched silently . . . as the tiers of lights dimmed slowly from white to yellow, then to red, and nothing was left but the murky mourning of the night, which hung over all like a pall."* Traveling with a U.S. unit, Gibbons later was wounded in France but recovered.

TOM GJELTEN (born 1948) is the national security correspondent for National Public Radio (NPR). He's reported on terrorism, espionage, and wars in Central America, Bosnia, Croatia, and the Persian Gulf. Here he captures some of the dangers war correspondents face in the twenty-first century. *"Various kinds of armed groups... make it clear to you right from the beginning what you can do.... Others are very chaotic, undisciplined, lawless.... All of a sudden you find yourself in a situation where... there don't seem to be any rules.... Those [situations] are, of course, much more dangerous... for a journalist."*

MARGUERITE HIGGINS (1920–1966) got stories that other reporters failed to get through sheer drive and personal courage. After covering World War II Europe, Higgins was sent to Korea to report on the war that had erupted there in 1950. She landed with the U.S. Marines at Inchon in September 1950 and sent home this account. *"I was with the fifth wave that hit "Red Beach."... We struck the sea wall hard at a place where it had crumbled into a canyon. The bullets were whining persistently, spattering the water around us. We clambered over the high steel sides of the boat, dropping into the water and, taking shelter beside the boat as long as we could, snaked on our stomachs up into a rock-strewn dip in the sea wall."*

MICHAEL KELLY (1957–2003) reported from the Gulf region in 1991 as a special correspondent of the *New Republic*. He was one of the few reporters in Baghdad when the bombing began. He was also in the first group of journalists to enter Kuwait City after its liberation. Here he marvels at the many ways Saddam Hussein was represented in Baghdad. *"There was a Saddam for every occasion, every location. In front of the Ministry of Justice, he wore judicial robes and held a scale; at the Ministry of Housing and Reconstruction, he had rolled up his sleeves to dig...; at the Ministry of Information and Culture, he worked at a desk, with pen and paper, and at the Ministry of Foreign Affairs, he smiled diplomatically in a pin-striped suit."* Kelly was killed in a vehicle accident in 2003, while covering the second war in Iraq.

GEORGE WILKINS KENDALL (1809–1867), a journalist and sheep rancher, founded the first cheap daily newspaper in New Orleans, the *Picayune*. (The name came from a small coin that had little value.) A supporter of U.S. victory in the Mexican-American War (1846–1848), Kendall traveled with the troops, filing dispatches during the Veracruz and Mexico City campaigns. This is from his account of the fall of Mexico City. *"Another victory, glorious in its results and which has thrown additional lustre upon the American arms, has been achieved to-day by the army under general [Winfield] Scott—the proud capital of Mexico has fallen into the power of a mere handful of men compared with the immense odds arrayed against them."*

HELEN KIRKPATRICK (1909–1997) was living in London in 1939, when World War II broke out in Europe. The *Chicago Daily News* hired her as its European correspondent, and she sent back eyewitness accounts that made her a celebrity in and around Chicago. Her picture was plastered on newsstands and buses. The paper referred to her as "our Helen" and urged readers to follow the war's progress by reading Kirkpatrick's articles. In 1940 Kirkpatrick described what happened during the German blitzkrieg after a German bomb hit a London hospital. *"In a bed on all that remains of the fourth story of the nurses' home of a big London hospital, a young nurse is pinned by a block [of concrete] which is holding up the wreckage of the floor above. Six men have been working since the early hours of this morning to lift the wreckage. . . . [They] are working against time—the remaining wall has a huge crack that is widening visibly by minutes and it is only a question of hours before it will crash."*

EDWARD R. MURROW  (1908–1965) headed the European bureau of CBS from 1937 to 1946. He became famous for his firsthand reports of life in Britain during World War II. Millions of Americans gathered around their radios to hear Murrow's rich voice describe the horrors of the German blitzkrieg and the bravery of British civilians and servicepeople. *"The air raid is still on . . . in London. . . . All night, for more than eight hours, the guns have been flashing. The blue of an autumn sky has been pockmarked with the small red burst of exploding antiaircraft shells. Never in the long history of this old city beside the Thames has there been such a night as this."*

DITH PRAN (born 1942) and **SYDNEY SCHANBERG** (born 1934)  teamed up in the 1970s to report on the Cambodian holocaust in which 1.7 million people—nearly one-fourth of the population—were put to death. From 1972 to 1975, they covered the civil war until the Communist Khmer Rouge took charge. Soon after the takeover, Khmer Rouge guerrillas arrested them. Pran's quick thinking convinced the young guerrillas that they were French, not U.S., journalists. *"They put guns to our heads and, shouting angrily, threatened us with execution. They took everything . . . and ordered us into an armored personnel carrier, slamming the hatch and rear door shut. We thought we were finished,"* Schanberg wrote. He escaped and went back to the United States. His coverage of the war won him a Pulitzer Prize, which he accepted for himself and Pran. Pran spent years in a brutal labor camp. He escaped to the United States in 1979. Schanberg's moving account, "The Death and Life of Dith Pran," appeared in the *New York Times* and was later made into the film, *The Killing Fields.* Pran has since devoted his life to making people aware of the Cambodian tragedy.

ERNIE PYLE (1900–1945) was one of the most honored war correspondents of World War II and was a huge favorite with U.S. GIs. Working for the *Washington Daily News*, Pyle traveled to London in 1940 to report on the German bombing raids. When Allied forces invaded Italy and France in 1944, Pyle was with them. He filed this report. *"Buck Eversole is a platoon sergeant in an infantry company. This means he has charge of about forty frontline fighting men. He has been at the front for more than a year. War is old to him and he has become a master of it. . . .' I know it ain't my fault that they get killed,' Buck finally said [about the boys under his command]. 'An' I do the best I can for them, but I've got so I feel like it's me killin' 'em instead of a German.'"*

Pyle also covered the fighting in the South Pacific, hopping from one island to the next with the U.S. Marines. Japanese machine-gun fire killed Pyle in 1945, and he was buried in a roadside grave with other Americans killed in action.

BERNARD SHAW (born 1940) rose through the ranks to become the principal Washington anchor for CNN. He spent the 1970s working for CBS and ABC, joining CNN in 1980. (He retired in 2001.) In 1989 he was in Beijing when the uprising at Tiananmen Square took place. He sent reports of the events, until the Chinese government forced CNN to stop its coverage. In 1991 Shaw and the other Boys of Baghdad brought live, around-the-clock news of the Allied bombing during Operation Desert Storm. On the impact of nearby explosions that swept through their hotel room, Shaw said, *"The skies over Baghdad have been illuminated. This is thunder, this is lightning, this is death—this is hell."*

 **BOB SIMON** (born 1941) has had a distinguished and award-winning career in journalism, covering military operations in Grenada, Somalia, Haiti, Northern Ireland, and the Falklands. CBS assigned him to cover the first Gulf War. Here he reports on what happened to him while he was imprisoned in Iraq. *"The canes were beating me on the head. There were two men doing the beating, one on either side of me.... I'd been beaten before; I'd been the victim of a mob before. But I'd never been systematically brutalized or tortured. The most frightening thing now was my sense that there were no limits. There was no code, no higher authority."* After his recovery, Simon continued on as a correspondent for CBS, especially for *60 Minutes II*. He is also a regular contributor to *60 Minutes* and the *CBS News.*

 **OLLIE STEWART** (1906–1977) was one of the most widely read African American correspondents during World War II. He covered the war's events in North Africa, Italy, France, and Germany for the *Baltimore Afro-American* and its affiliated newspapers. Stewart entered Paris in September 1944, although there were still pockets of German resistance in the city. He wrote, *"As our jeep stopped, a stuttering machine gun on the roof sprayed the street, and on the opposite corner another opened up. I crossed several open corners that were being crisscrossed by fire coming from rooftops and windows. I finally crawled under a tank at an intersection where a girl was bleeding and a baby crying as rifles, pistols and grenades took up a refrain that echoed throughout the city."*

WALLACE TERRY (1938–2003) was deputy bureau chief for *Time* magazine in Saigon from 1967 to 1969. He was the first African American war correspondent to represent the mainstream media and the only journalist to write of the experiences of black soldiers. Terry later won wide praise for his best-selling book, *Bloods: An Oral History of the Vietnam War by Black Veterans*, published in 1984. The book, Terry said, showed that *"the black experience is first and foremost a universal experience,"* adding, *"These men learned that an enemy bullet does not discriminate."*

HENRY VILLARD (1835–1900), born in Germany, arrived in the United States at the age of eighteen and spent time in Cincinnati and Chicago before becoming a correspondent for a German newspaper in New York. In this job, he reported on the debates between Abraham Lincoln and Stephen Douglas during the 1860 presidential election. During the Civil War (1861-1865), he became a correspondent for the *New York Herald* and later the *New York Tribune*. This is from his dispatch for the *Herald* that he filed from Centerville, Virginia, on July 19, 1861, during the Bull Run campaign. *"The representatives of the press stood their ground as well as any, in spite of the shot, shell, and rifle balls that kept whizzing past them for hours."*

Source Notes

2 *War Stories: Reporting in the Time of Conflict from the Crimea to Iraq* (Boston: Bunker Hill Publishing, 2003), 7.

6 Aine Cryts, "CNN's Christiane Amanpour Receives Goldsmith Career Award," *The John F. Kennedy School of Government, Harvard University*, March 13, 2002, http://www.ksg.harvard.edu/news/news/2002/amanpour_goldsmithawards_031302.htm (April 15, 2005).

7 "Covering All Bases: Patriotism, Objectivity, and the Pursuit of Journalism in Wartime," *U.S. News & World Report*, November 9, 2001, 44.

7 "Critics of War Say Lack of Scrutiny Helped Administration to Press Its Case," *New York Times*, March 23, 2003, B10.

10 *The World Book Encyclopedia*, Vol. 4, "Constitution of the United States" (Chicago: World Book, Inc., 2000), 1011.

11 Philip Knightley, *The First Casualty: The War Correspondent as Hero and Myth-Maker from the Crimea to Kosovo* (Baltimore: Johns Hopkins University Press, 2002), vii.

12 "Philip Knightley on War Reporting," Talking Point: Forum, *BBC News*, October 23, 2001, http://newswww.bbc.net.uk/1/low/talking_point/forum/1604226.stm (April 15, 2005).

12 Cryts, "CNN's Christiane Amanpour."

12 Ibid.

13 Knightley, *First Casualty*, 2.

14 James M. Perry, *A Bohemian Brigade: The Civil War Correspondents, Mostly Rough, Sometimes Ready* (New York: John Wiley & Sons, Inc., 2000), 31–32.

15 Knightley, *First Casualty*, 58.

16 Nathaniel Lande, *Dispatches from the Front: A History of the American War Correspondent* (New York: Oxford University Press, 1996), 52.

17 Knightley, *First Casualty*, 19.

17 Mary Beth North, David M. Katzman, Paul D. Escott, Howard P. Chudacoff, Thomas G. Paterson, and William M. Tittle Jr., *A People and a Nation: A History of the United States*, 4th ed. (Boston: Houghton Mifflin Co., 1994), 273.

17 Knightley, *First Casualty*, 21.

18 Ibid.

19 Donald A. Ritchie, *American Journalists: Getting the Story* (New York: Oxford University Press, 1997), 19.

20 Knightley, *First Casualty*, 58.

23 Ibid, 126.

24 Ibid, 133.

26 "The New York Philharmonic," *CBS Radio Network*, recording, December 7, 1941, accessed at the Museum of Radio and TV, October 4, 2002.

31 Ibid.

32 "Ernie Pyle," *Indiana Historical Society*, n.d., http://www.indianahistory.org/heritage (August 30, 2002).

33 Knightley, *First Casualty*, 357.

34 Frederick S. Voss, *Reporting the War, The Journalistic Coverage of World War II* (Washington, DC: Smithsonian Press, 1994), 57.

35 Tad Bartimus, "Bullets and Bathrooms," in *Media Studies Journal: Front Lines and Deadlines, Perspectives on War Reporting* (Arlington, VA: The Freedom Forum, 2001), 9.

37 Voss, *Reporting the War*, 23–24.

40 Martin Luther King Jr., "Remarks for Negro Newspaper Week," *The Papers of Martin Luther King Jr.*, February 10, 1958, http://www.stanford.edu/group/King/publications/papers/vol4/580210-001-Remarks_for_Negro_Press_Week.htm (April 15, 2005).

43 Penny Colman, *Where the Action Was: Women Correspondents in World War II* (New York: Crown, 2002), 99.

44 Ibid.

45 Knightley, *First Casualty*, 360.

46–47 Ibid., 329.

48 Ibid.

48 Ibid.

48 Voss, *Reporting the War*, 208.

50 Jon E. Lewis, ed., *The Mammoth Book of War Correspondents* (New York: Carroll & Graf Publishers, Inc., 2001), 435.

52 Ritchie, *American Journalists*, 276.

52 Knightley, *First Casualty*, 366.

52 Ibid.

53 Ibid., 367.

53 Ibid.

53 Ibid.

53 Ibid.

54 Ritchie, *American Journalists*, 276.

58 Edward Wakin, *How TV Changed America's Mind* (New York: Lothrup, Lee and Sheperd, 1996), 38.

58 Ibid.

58 Ibid.

58 Ibid.

60 Lewis, *Mammoth*, 490.

61 Jane E. Kirtley, "Enough Is Enough," in *Media Studies Journal, "Frontlines and Deadlines, Perspectives on War Reporting,"* (Arlington, VA: The Freedom Forum, 2001), 41.

63 Knightley, *First Casualty*, 416.

65 Natalie Cortes, "Danger, Grief, Betrayal Mark Reporters Time in Vietnam" n.d., http://freedomforum .org (March 16, 2005).

65–66 Tad Bartimus, ed., *War Torn: Stories of War from the Women Reporters Who Covered Vietnam.* (New York: Random House, 2002), vii.

66 Ibid., 151.

67 Ibid.

68 John R. MacArthur, *Second Front: Censorship and Propaganda in the Gulf War* (Berkeley: University of California Press, 1992), 134.

68 Wakin, *How TV Changed*, 79.

69 Peter Braestrap, "Myths and Realities, The News Media and the War in Vietnam," n.d., http://www.vwam .com/vets/media.htm, (September 9, 2002).

72 Lewis, *Mammoth*, 594–595.

74 Knightley, *First Casualty*, 484.

79 Eric Schmitt, "Five Years Later, the Gulf War Story Is Still Being Told," *New York Times*, May 12, 1996, 241–247.

79 "John Holliman, 49, of CNN; Covered '91 Baghdad Attack," *New York Times*, September 9, 1998, Section 1, 63.

80 Knightley, *First Casualty*, 493.

80 Ibid.

80 Bob Frost, "The West Interview," Peter Arnett, April 10, 1994, http://www.bobfrost.com/west/ arnett.html (August 30, 2002), 2–3.

82 "'Boys of Baghdad' Relive Gulf War Broadcast," CNN.com, January 17, 2003, http://www.cnn.com/2003/US/ 01/16/cnna.shaw.arnett (March 25, 2005).

82 "Bush Tells the Military to Get Ready; Long Battle Seen," *New York Times*, September 16, 2001, 1.

86–87 Kim Campbell, "Today's War Reporting: It's Digital, but Dangerous," *Christian Science Monitor*, December 4, 2001, http://www.csmonitor.com/ 2001 (September 12, 2002).

87 "Geraldo Draws Fire, Figuratively: Does His Posturing Increase the Danger to Other Journalists in a Perilous Place?" December 17, 2001,

http://www.findarticles.com (September 1, 2002).

88 "Daniel Pearl: Seeker for Dialogue," *BBC News*, February 21, 2002, http://www.news.bbc.co.uk/1/hi/world/south_asia/1793670.stm (April 18, 2005).

89 "When Kidnappers Issued Ultimatum, Reporters Did the Opposite," *ABCNews.com*, January 31, 2002 (November 25, 2002).

89 "Protecting the Press: Journalists in War Zones," *School of Communications, American University, Washington, D.C.*, April 3, 2002, http://www.soc.american.edu/main.cfm?pageid=495 (April 15, 2005).

90 Timothy Carlson and Bill Katovsky, Embedded: *The Media at War in Iraq* (Guilford, CT: The Lyons Press, 2003), 177.

91 Andrew Jacobs, "My Weekend at Embed Boot Camp," *New York Times* Magazine, March 2, 2003, 91.

94 "In an F-18, Five Seconds from a Deck Veiled by a Sandstorm." *New York Times*, March 27, 2003, B5.

94 "Reporters Respond Eagerly to Pentagon Welcome Mat," *New York Times*, March 23, 2003, B3.

95 Ibid.

95 Ibid.

97 "Arnett Is Dismissed by NBC after Remarks on Iraqi TV," *New York Times*, April 1. 2003, B14.

97 "Bush Declares 'One Victory in War on Terror,'" *New York Times*, May 2, 2003, A1.

97 "Even Critics of War Say White House Spun It with Skill," *New York Times*, April 20, 2003, B14.

101 "Get Me Rewrite, Now Bullets Are Flying," *New York Times*, October 10, 2004, 4.

102 "In Iraq Election, Tense Media Put on Short Leash," *New York Observer*, January 31, 2005, 21.

102 "Under Threat: Iraq Journalists Frequently Face Hazardous Conditions on the Job," *Committee to Protect Journalists*, May 17, 2004, http://www.cpj.org (February 25, 2005).

102 "Did Media Target Journalists in Iraq?" *Christian Science Monitor*, February 18, 2005, http://www.csmonitor.com (February 25, 2005).

103 Ibid.

103 Committee to Protect Journalists, *On Assignment: A Guide to Reporting in Dangerous Situations* (Washington, DC: Committee to Protect Journalists, n.d.), 4.

103 Ibid.

104 Ibid.

106 "Tyranny of the Taliban," *Time*, October 13, 1997, 60.

106 *Chicago Tribune*, April 30, 1975.

107 Betsy Wade, ed., *Forward Positions: The War Correspondence of Homer Bigart* (Fayetteville: University of Arkansas Press, 1992), 148.

107 Margaret Bourke-White, *Portrait of Myself* (New York: Simon and Schuster, 1963), 258–259.

108 "Who, What, When, Why?" *CBS Report*, February 27, 1968.

108 Lande, *Dispatches*, 141.

108–109 Michelle Ferrari, comp., "Gloria Emerson, Life in Saigon," *Reporting America at War: An Oral History*, http://www.pbs.org/weta/reportingamericaatwar/reporters/emerson/saigon.html (April 15, 2005).

109 *The Columbia World of Quotations*, Columbia University Press, 1996. http://www.barleby.com/66/88/24588.html (April 12, 2005).

109 *Chicago Tribune*, February 26, 1917.

110 *War Stories*, 17.

110 *New York Herald-Tribune*, September 18, 1950.

110 Michael Kelly, *Martyrs' Day: Chronicle of a Small War* (New York: Random House, 1993), 35.

111 Lande, *Dispatches*, 82.

111 Colman, *Where the Action Was*, 17.

112 "Edward R. Murrow," *CBS Radio Network*, audio recording of radio broadcast of September 11, 1940; accessed at the Museum of Radio and TV, October 4, 2002.

112 Lewis, *Mammoth*, 558–559.

113 *Washington Times*, February 22, 1944.

113 "Bernard Shaw Retires (Transcript)," *CNN.com*, November 20, 2000, http://www.sfu.ca/~joes/jnn/cnn _features/bernard.html (March 28, 2005).

114 Bob Simon, *Forty Days* (New York: G. P. Putnam's, 1992), 41.

114 Ollie Stewart, "Invasion of France," in *This Is Our War*, http://www.afro.com/ history/OurWar/stewart (March 11, 2005).

115 Wallace Terry, '59, "BAM, 100 Years of Distinction," November/December 2000, http://www.brown.edu/ Administration/Brown_Alumni _Magazine/01/11-00./features journalism.html (March 11, 2005).

115 Lande, *Dispatches*, 106.

Selected Bibliography

Arnett, Peter. *Live from the Battlefield: From Vietnam to Baghdad, 35 Years in the World's War Zones.* New York, Simon & Schuster, 1994.

Bartimus, Tad, ed. *War Torn: Stories of War from the Women Who Covered Vietnam.* New York: Random House, 2002.

Benson, Sonia. *Korean War: Almanac and Primary Sources.* Detroit: Gale, 2001.

Blondheim, Menahem. *News Over Wires: The Telegraph and the Flow of Public Information in America, 1844–1897.* Cambridge, MA: Harvard University Press, 1994.

Blow, Michael. *A Ship to Remember: The Maine and the Spanish-American War.* New York: William Morrow, 1992.

Browne, Malcolm W. *Muddy Boots and Red Socks: A Reporter's Life.* New York: Times Books, 1993.

Burg, David. *The American Revolution: An Eyewitness History*. New York: Library of American History, 2001.

Colman, Penny. *Where the Action Was: Women War Correspondents in World War II*. New York: Crown, 2002.

Cronkite, Walter. *A Reporter's Life*. New York: Ballantine Books, 1997.

Emerson, Gloria. *Winners & Losers: Battles, Retreats, Gains, Losses, and Ruins from the Vietnam War*. New York: W. W. Norton, 1992.

Gellhorn, Martha. *The Face of War*. New York: Atlantic Monthly Press, 1988.

Hallin, Daniel C. *The "Uncensored War": The Media and Vietnam*. Berkeley: University of California Press, 1989.

Heinz, W. C. *When We Were One: Stories of World War II*. Cambridge, MA: Da Capo Books, 2002.

Kelly, Michael. *Martyr's Day: Chronicle of a Small War*. New York: Random House, 1993.

Knightley, Philip. *The First Casualty: The War Correspondent as Hero and Myth Maker from the Crimea to Kosovo*. Rev. Ed. Baltimore: Johns Hopkins University Press, 2002.

Lande, Nathaniel. *Dispatches from the Front: News Accounts of American Wars, 1776–1991*. New York: Henry Holt, 1995.

Lewis, Jon E., ed. *The Mammoth Book of War Correspondents*. New York: Carroll & Graf Publishers, Inc., 2001.

MacArthur, John R. *Second Front: Censorship and Propaganda in the Gulf War*. New York: Hill and Wang, 1992.

McLaughlin, Greg. *The War Correspondent*. Sterling, VA: Pluto Press, 2002.

Media Studies Journal: Front Lines and Deadlines, Perspectives on War Reporting. Arlington, VA: The Freedom Forum, 2001.

Nichols, David, ed. *Ernie's War: The Best of Ernie Pyle's World War II Dispatches.* New York: Random House, 1986.

Perry, James M. *A Bohemian Brigade: The Civil War Correspondents, Mostly Rough, Sometimes Ready.* New York: John Wiley & Sons, Inc., 2000.

Reporting Vietnam: Part One, American Journalism, 1959–1969; Part Two, American Journalism, 1969–1975. New York: Library of America, 1998.

Reporting World War II, Part One, American Journalism, 1938–1944; Part Two, American Journalism, 1944–1946. New York: Library of America, 1995.

Robertson, James I. Jr. *Civil War! America Becomes One Nation.* New York: Alfred A. Knopf, 1992.

Roth, Mitchel P. *Historical Dictionary of War Journalism.* Westport, CT: Greenwood Press, 1997.

Simon, Bob. *Forty Days.* New York: G. P. Putnam's, 1992.

Voss, Frederick S. *Reporting the War: The Journalistic Coverage of World War II.* Washington, DC: Smithsonian Press, 1994.

Warren, James A. *Portrait of Tragedy: America and the Vietnam War.* New York: Lothrop, Lee, and Shepherd, 1990.

Zeinert, Karen. *Those Extraordinary Women of World War I.* Brookfield, CT: The Millbrook Press, 2001.

Zeinert, Karen, and Mary Miller. *The Brave Women of the Gulf Wars: Operation Desert Storm and Operation Iraqi Freedom.* Minneapolis: Twenty-First Century Books, 2006.

Further Reading and Websites

BOOKS

Armstrong, Jennifer. *Photo by Brady: A Picture of the Civil War.* New York: Atheneum, 2005.

Arnold, James R. *The Civil War.* Minneapolis: Lerner Publications Company, 2005.

Dolan, Edward F. *The Spanish-American War.* Brookfield, CT: The Millbrook Press, 2001.

Feldman, Ruth Tenzer. *The Korean War.* Minneapolis: Lerner Publications Company, 2004.

Furbee, Mary Rodd. *Outrageous Women of Civil War Times.* Hoboken: John Wiley and Sons, 2003.

Goldstein, Margaret. *Word War II: Europe.* Minneapolis: Lerner Publications Company, 2004.

Hamilton, John. *Real-Time Reporting.* Edina, MN: ABDO and Daughters, 2004.

Levy, Debbie. *The Vietnam War.* Minneapolis: Lerner Publications Company, 2004.

McGowen, Thomas. *Air Raid! The Bombing Campaigns of World War II.* Brookfield, CT: The Millbrook Press, 2001.

Morrison, Taylor. *Civil War Artist.* Boston: Houghton Mifflin, 1999.

O'Connor, Barbara. *The Soldiers' Voice: The Story of Ernie Pyle.* Minneapolis: Carolrhoda Books, Inc., 1996.

Welch, Catherine A. *Margaret Bourke-White: Racing with a Dream.* Minneapolis : Carolrhoda Books, Inc., 1998.

Williams, Barbara. *World War II: Pacific.* Minneapolis: Lerner Publications Company, 2004.

Zeinert, Karen. *Those Courageous Women of the Civil War.* Brookfield, CT: The Millbrook Press, 1998.

Zwier, Lawrence J., and Matthew S. Weltig. *The Persian Gulf and Iraqi Wars.* Minneapolis: Lerner Publications Company, 2005.

WEBSITES

Committee to Protect Journalists. http://www.cpj.org. The Committee to Protect Journalists is a nonprofit organization dedicated to the defense of press freedom.

Institute for War and Peace Reporting (IWPR). http://www.iwpr.net/home_index_new.html. IWPR is dedicated to the training of war and peace correspondents and the reporting of accurate, timely news.

Newseum. http://www.newseum.org/warstories. This interactive online exhibit by Newseum offers visitors information about the history of war correspondence, including audio interviews with reporters, an annotated timeline of media technology used during war, field photographs, and more.

Reporters without Borders. http://www.rsf.org. Reporters without Borders is an international organization that seeks to provide for the safety of journalists who are working in war zones or other dangerous areas.

Usnewsclassroom.com. http://www.usnewsclassroom.com/resources/activities/war_reporting/index. html. Students and teachers will find helpful information about one hundred years of war correspondence, its dangers and issues. The site includes text, photographs, reporter profiles, as well as have access to an online question-and-answer interface with a field reporter.

Places to Visit

Ernie Pyle State Historic Site
Dana, Indiana 47847
Telephone: (765) 665-3633
Website: http://www.scripps.com/foundation/programs/pyle/pyle.html

Freedom Forum Journalists Memorial
1101 Wilson Boulevard
Arlington, Virginia 22209
Telephone: (703) 284-3544
Website: http://www.freedomforum.org

Museum of Television & Radio
25 West 52nd Street
New York, New York 10019
Telephone: (212) 621-6600

465 North Beverly Drive
Beverly Hills, California 90210
Telephone: (310) 786-1000
Website: http://www.mtr.org

The Newseum (to open in 2007)
Sixth Street and Pennsylvania Avenue NW
Washington, D.C.
Website: http://www.newseum.org

Index

Photo Acknowledgments

The images in this book are used with the permission of: © Nicholas Kamm/AFP/Getty Images, p. 6; National Archives, pp. 8, 33, 34, 43 (United States Holocaust Memorial Museum), 45 [111-SC-201615], 52, 64, 67 (United States Department of Defense), 107 (bottom) [208-PU-2215-3], 111, 113; George E. Sullivan, pp. 9, 17, 110; Library of Congress, pp. 11 [LC-USZ62-66061], 16 [LC-USZ72-14216], 19 [LC-B8171-0245], 21 [LC-USZ62-80], 24 [LC-USZ62-21728], 36 [LC-USZ62-100537], 39, 58 [LC-USZ62-100016], 108 (bottom) [LC-USZ62-103860], 109 [LC-USZ62-127902], 112 (top) [LC-USZ62-126483]; © Medford Historical Society Collection/CORBIS, p. 14; © Bettmann/CORBIS, pp. 23, 25, 50, 60, 72, 107 (top), 112 (bottom); © Brown Brothers, pp. 26, 115 (bottom); AP/Wide World Photos, pp. 28, 29, 42, 47, 54, 62, 66, 75, 77, 82, 86, 88, 91, 106 (bottom); Syracuse University Library, p. 44; © Todd Strand/Independent Picture Service, courtesy Random House, Inc./Knopf Publishing Group, p. 48; courtesy Tisch Library, Tufts University, p. 57; UPI Photo by Kyoichi Sawada, p. 69; © CBS Photo Archive, pp. 78, 108 (top); Sgt. Joseph R. Chenelly/U.S. Marines, p. 85; Sgt. Daryl G. Sanford, USMC/United States Department of Defense, p. 90; © CNN, p. 93; © NBC-TV, p. 96; © AFP/Stephen Jaffe/Getty Images, p. 98; © AMMAR AWAD/Reuters/CORBIS, p. 101; © Olivier Coret/In Visu/CORBIS, p. 104; © Erik S. Lesser/Getty Images, p. 106 (top); The Moorland-Spingarn Research Center, Howard University, p. 114; courtesy Brown University, p. 115 (top).

Cover: Sgt. Daryl G. Sanford, USMC/United States Department of Defense

Titles from the Award-Winning People's History Series:

Accept No Substitutes! The History of American Advertising

Declaring Independence: Life during the American Revolution

Don't Whistle in School: The History of America's Public Schools

Dressed for the Occasion: What Americans Wore 1620–1970

Failure Is Impossible! The History of American Women's Rights

The Fight for Peace: A History of Antiwar Movements in America

Good Women of a Well-Blessed Land: Women's Lives in Colonial America

Headin' for Better Times: The Arts of the Great Depression

Into the Land of Freedom: African Americans in Reconstruction

Journalists at Risk: Reporting America's Wars

Thar She Blows: American Whaling in the Nineteenth Century

We Shall Overcome: The History of the American Civil Rights Movement

What's Cooking? The History of American Food